TRADITIONAL

BRITISH
COOKING

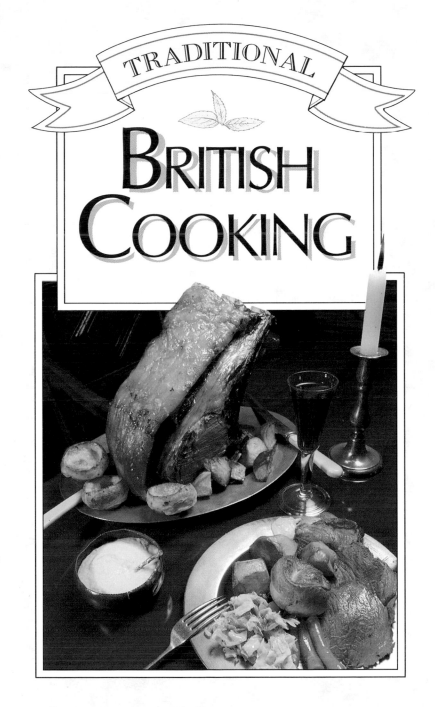

Photographed by Peter Barry
Designed by Lone Orpin and Helen Johnson
Edited by Jillian Stewart and Kate Cranshaw
Introduction by Roz Cocks

3395
This edition published in 1994 by
Tiger Books International PLC, London
© 1994 CLB Publishing, Godalming, Surrey
Printed and bound in Singapore
ISBN 1-85501-397-5

TRADITIONAL

BRITISH COOKING

TIGER BOOKS INTERNATIONAL
LONDON

Introduction

Traditional British cooking stems from a less stressful age, when ingredients were simple, but wholesome and good, and cooking methods were unhurried. In retrospect, this way of life sounds relaxing and good for the soul as opposed to the frenetic rushing in and out grabbing of snacks and microwaved freezer foods that has sadly become a way of life for many people today. Of course, it was not really such an idyll. There was undoubtedly a lot of hard graft involved in the chopping of vegetables, mixing of pastries and cakes, and the beating of batters and sponges, all without today's modern electrical equipment.

To return entirely to this way of life would be unrealistic and undesirable for most of us, but it is not difficult to extract and adapt the essence of what was best about traditional British food in the past, namely the fresh, simple ingredients and wholesome recipes, and to incorporate them into modern life. The benefits are manifold – the ingredients are always easy to obtain, the methods are much quicker with modern kitchen equipment, and most importantly you feel like you are eating 'real' food that is satisfying and delicious.

To appreciate our very broad culinary heritage, it is necessary to go back in time and pick up the various strands that came together to form British cooking. The Celts who came from Europe in 700BC were the first civilising influence to come to British shores. They organised farms around a central eating hall, and so raised eating into a sociable occasion. They grew wheat, ground it into flour and baked it into bread in earth ovens. They kept cows, pigs and sheep, made butter and cheese, and brewed beer from barley. In fact it was the Celts who first set a pattern to British food.

The Romans were on British soil for 400 years, and introduced a number of foods to our shores, including rabbits, pheasants and guinea fowl; a variety of cultivated fruit and vegetables including apples, pears, peas, onions and lettuce; and lots of herbs and spices, notably rosemary, sage, thyme, mint, parsley, ginger, garlic and pepper. The Angles, Jutes, Saxons and Danes, who invaded our eastern coasts from Holland, Germany and Scandinavia, brought their Nordic methods of salting and smoking fish and meat, which persist to this day in the form of hams, bacon and smoked fish. The Danes devised these methods out of necessity to enable them to keep meat and fish through their long winters, and during their adventurous sea voyages.

Our last invaders, the Normans, who arrived with William the Conqueror in the eleventh century, introduced cider-making and many new flavourings and spices. British adventurers in Elizabethan times brought back foods such as tomatoes and potatoes that were to change the British diet for ever. British colonisation of the West Indies, West Africa, South Africa and the Far East yielded great quantities of sugar, cocoa, citrus and dried fruit, spices and also exotic fruits. These ingredients from foreign shores enhanced and complemented our own indigenous produce, and British cooking took on a new sophistication.

Our temperate isles are richly endowed with the essential elements necessary for the husbandry of many and varied crops and livestock. Ireland's lush pastures feed dairy cattle that are famous for producing creamy milk and cheeses, and potatoes also grow magnificently here due to the mild, wet climate. Scottish beef cattle, especially Aberdeen Angus, are prized for their good-flavoured meat. The gently rolling hills of Wales and the North and South Downs of Kent and Sussex provide just the right terrain for the sheep that also yield famously sweet meat.

The flat and fertile plains of Norfolk and Suffolk are perfect for wheat growing and produce a wealth of market garden crops, while the sunny valleys of Herefordshire and Kent produce an abundance of lovely fruits. Kent is known as 'The Garden of England' and gives forth beautiful tasty apples, juicy pears, crimson cherries and many varieties of strawberries. The Aberdeen area, in Scotland, is home to most of Britain's raspberries. The wildness of Scotland, in terms of climate and landscape, is good for the growing of oats and for the catching of game birds such as partridge, woodcock and pheasant, and for fishing, which brings us the delicate flavours of salmon and trout.

Not only is Britain's land bountiful, our seas are teeming with good things to eat, too. Our fishermen bring in cod, plaice and haddock – all famous with chips, and delicious turbot, halibut and Dover sole. Dover sole is as fine a fish as can be found anywhere, and is particularly highly prized. Herring and mackerel, both oily fish, have long been British favourites, too. Shellfish, too, are abundant in our waters: there are lobsters, crabs, crawfish, prawns, shrimps, oysters, mussels, cockles, scallops and whelks, all there for the catching.

Thus, there is clearly no excuse for the British not to eat exceedingly well and that is what traditional British cooking is all about. It calls for quality locally-produced ingredients married, when necessary, with colonial spice. Our recipes are solid and satisfying, but often have that important extra ingredient, such as wine, beer, cider, ground nuts, cinnamon, cloves, nutmeg or mustard, which elevates the everyday basic ingredients into special and memorable meals.

Breakfast in its traditional British form is famous the world over. It is highly nutritious and fortifying and prepares the eater for an energetic day's work or play. Porridge comes first, either with a sprinkling of salt if you are serving it the traditional Scottish way, and sugar if you are not. This can be replaced with half a grapefruit, carefully loosened from its skin and pith. Bacon and eggs are a must, with the eggs carefully fried, poached or scrambled, toast and marmalade follow, and all this is complemented with steaming tea or coffee. Salt, pepper and English mustard should also be on the table. These are the bare bones of this wonderful meal for which visitors come from all corners of the earth to sample.

There are many breakfast variations, such as boiled eggs, or a mixed grill with bacon, eggs, tomatoes and mushrooms, or sausages, and many people like kippers with thinly sliced brown bread and butter, or even a plate of kedgeree. In Ireland freshly baked soda bread is a wonderful accompaniment to the bacon and eggs, and is the ideal mopper-up of egg and bacon fat. Herrings in oatmeal and oatcakes are two further Scottish breakfast specialities. This is not the version of breakfast that most people have time for during the week, and indeed it is probably not the healthiest meal by modern standards if you have a sedentary job, say in an office. However, at weekends it makes a pleasant leisurely start that sets one up for a long morning of activity.

Following such a substantial breakfast, the main meal of the day is unlikely to be at midday, but rather at the end of the day, once the day's activity is over. The names given to British mealtimes is a study in itself, and reflects the different working patterns and class cultures embraced by British society. The second most important British mealtime after breakfast is tea. This can mean one of a number of things. Tea can be, at its most elevated, an elegant drawing-room affair with delicately cut cucumber sandwiches, scones and Devonshire cream and a fine fruit cake or sponge set on a pedestal plate, accompanied by good Indian tea poured into fine bone china cups. This is usually served around 4 p.m. Like breakfast, this sort of tea is an informal mealtime where people can help themselves to what they want, and there is no pressure to eat everything on offer. Nowadays it is more usual to have a plate of scones, or just a freshly baked cake at tea, rather than so many different items. British cakes have an essential simplicity about them that sets them apart from their many-layered and rather rich continental counterparts. This sort of tea is usually followed by an evening meal at about 8 or 9 p.m.

Tea can also mean the main evening meal, eaten at 5 or 6 p.m. soon after the working members of the household return home. There is also high tea, which is the name given to a light evening meal with savoury and sweet dishes, and tea to drink. Supper can be a snack, such as bread and cheese, eaten late in the evening, or it can mean a light evening meal. Dinner can mean a substantial midday meal, as in school dinner, or it can mean a sophisticated evening 3-course affair. Lunch, it is reasonably safe to say, is always in the middle of the day, but can certainly vary tremendously in content and size from a sandwich to a grand and formal many-coursed occasion.

A traditional British main meal, be it lunch or evening dinner, consists of a soup or other starter, a fish, meat, poultry or game main dish accompanied by suitable vegetables, followed by a dessert and then cheese, or at a very grand meal a savoury can be served at the end of a meal instead of cheese.

The French, who serve cheese after the main course and before the dessert find our habits curious. In Britain this custom of finishing the meal on a savoury note stems from not wishing to start on the port, which would always be handed round at the end of a formal evening meal, with a sweet taste in the mouth.

This is a book of lovely soups, piquant starters, simply cooked fish, hearty game dishes, meat puddings, pies and pasties, sticky and sinful puddings and wonderful teatime specialities. They are classic British recipes that have an uncomplicated elegance, are suitable for all occasions and are sure to delight cook, as well as family and friends.

CONTENTS

CHAPTER ONE

SOUPS
&
STARTERS

POTATO SOUP

*Originally brought to Britain from Spain in the early 1600s,
the humble potato was soon recognised as an important staple.
Although not widely accepted at first, they eventually found their way
into a diverse array of recipes ranging from soups to scones.*

SERVES 8-10

INGREDIENTS

*900g/2lbs potatoes
2 onions
1 small carrot
60g/2oz butter
1.14 litres/2 pints vegetable or chicken stock
Bay leaf, sprig of parsley and thyme
570ml/1 pint milk
Salt and pepper
Cream and chives, for garnish*

1 Peel and dice the potatoes and slice the onions and carrot. Melt the butter in a large saucepan and soften the onions in it.

2 Add the potatoes and carrot and stir in the stock and herbs. Cover and bring to the boil, then reduce the heat and simmer for 30 minutes.

3 Push the vegetables through a sieve or vegetable mill or blend them in a liquidiser or food processor.

4 Add the milk to the purée and return the mixture to the pan, simmering for another 30 minutes.

5 Season well before serving, adding some cream if wished, and garnish each serving with chives.

Cook's Notes

Time
Preparation takes 15 minutes and cooking takes 1 hour.

Variation
The onions may be replaced with leeks.

CULLEN SKINK

*Finnan haddock was traditionally used
for this creamy Scottish broth or 'Skink'
from the village of Cullen.*

<u>SERVES 4</u>

INGREDIENTS

460g/1lb smoked haddock fillets, skinned
570ml/1 pint fish stock
225g/8oz potatoes, peeled and diced
1 onion, chopped
2 sticks celery, diced
Salt and pepper
280ml/½ pint milk
140ml/¼ pint single cream
2 hard-boiled eggs, chopped
2 tbsps chopped parsley

1 Place the fish in a shallow saucepan and pour over enough of the stock to just cover. Bring to the boil and simmer gently for about 10 minutes or until the fish is cooked through.

2 Remove the fish from the stock and flake it finely, discarding any bones. Reserve the stock.

3 Place the potatoes, onion, celery, reserved stock and remaining stock in a large saucepan. Simmer for about 20 minutes until tender then purée in a food processor or liquidiser.

4 Return the puréed mixture to the pan with the milk and bring to the boil. Reduce the heat to a simmer and add the fish and cream. Heat through and serve. Garnish each serving with some of the chopped hard-boiled eggs and parsley.

Cook's Notes

Time
Preparation takes 10 minutes and cooking takes about 40 minutes.

Variation
A little white wine may be added in place of some of the stock.

Preparation
Once the cream has been added do not allow the soup to boil.

SCOTCH BROTH

A classic one-pot meal, the broth
can be served separately from the meat.

SERVES 8

INGREDIENTS

900g/2lb scrag end of lamb, trimmed
1.7 litres/3 pints water
90g/3oz pearl barley
Salt and pepper
1 onion, chopped
1 large carrot, peeled and sliced
1 small swede, peeled and diced
1 leek, trimmed, washed and sliced
2 sticks celery, sliced
Chopped parsley, to garnish

1 Place the lamb and water in a large saucepan and bring to the boil. Skim off any scum that forms.

2 Stir in the barley and seasoning, and reduce the heat. Cover and simmer for 1½ hours.
3 Add the prepared vegetables to the pan and continue to simmer gently for another 1½ hours. Occasionally, skim off the fat as it rises to the surface.
4 Using a slotted spoon, remove the lamb from the pan and allow to cool slightly. Remove the meat from the bones and discard the bones and any fat or gristle.
5 Cut the meat into small pieces and return to the pan. Simmer for a further 30 minutes or until the meat is completely reheated.
6 Season to taste and serve garnished with a sprinkling of chopped parsley.

Cook's Notes

Time
Preparation takes 20 minutes and cooking takes 3½ hours.

Variation
Use whatever vegetables are in season.

WATERCRESS SOUP

*One of our tastiest salad vegetables, watercress is not only
rich in flavour, it is also a valuable source of iron and vitamins.
Hampshire is an area which has grown watercress for many
generations and this delicious recipe from the region is a perfect
example of why watercress has continued to grow in popularity.*

<u>SERVES 4-6</u>

INGREDIENTS

2 large bunches fresh watercress
45g/1½oz butter
1 small onion, chopped
30g/1oz plain flour
700ml/1½ pints chicken or vegetable stock
3-4 sprigs parsley, chopped
Salt and pepper
420ml/¾ pint milk

1 Wash and pick over the watercress, discarding any
yellow leaves. Reserve enough sprigs for garnish and
chop the remaining watercress roughly.

2 Melt the butter in a saucepan and cook the onion
for 3 minutes without browning. Add the watercress
and continue cooking over a gentle heat for another
4 minutes, stirring constantly to avoid browning.
3 Sprinkle in the flour and blend in well. Gradually stir
in the stock and bring to the boil. Add the parsley and
seasoning, reduce heat and simmer for 15 minutes.
4 Cool slightly and blend until smooth. Add the milk
and reheat. Adjust the seasoning. Garnish each serving
with the reserved watercress.

Cook's Notes

Time
Preparation takes 20
minutes and cooking takes
about 25 minutes.

Serving Idea
Serve hot or cold
with swirls of cream.

Variation
Add some diced
potatoes to the soup and
simmer for about 45
minutes.

19

CREAM OF CARROT SOUP

Carrots have long been considered a popular and versatile vegetable. In the past they have even been used in place of fresh fruit in many sweet recipes, as their natural sweetness lent itself quite easily to many desserts – hence the evolution of carrot cake.

SERVES 4

INGREDIENTS

1 tbsp oil
1 large onion, chopped
460g/1lb carrots, chopped
1 tsp mixed herbs
850ml/1½ pints chicken or vegetable stock
140ml/¼ pint soured cream
Salt and pepper

1 Heat the oil in a large saucepan and sauté the chopped onion until transparent.

2 Add the carrots, mixed herbs and stock.
3 Bring to the boil then reduce the heat and simmer for about 30 minutes, or until the carrots are soft.
4 Cool a little and then blend in a liquidiser or food processor until smooth.
5 Add the soured cream, season to taste and mix thoroughly. Heat through gently and serve.

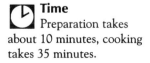

Cook's Notes

Time
Preparation takes about 10 minutes, cooking takes 35 minutes.

Watchpoint
Do not allow the soup to boil after adding the soured cream.

Variation
For a richer soup, omit the soured cream and add a swirl of double cream just before serving.

LEEK SOUP

This Welsh soup is traditionally served with a piece of Caerphilly cheese on the side.

<u>SERVES 4-6</u>

INGREDIENTS

4 rashers back bacon, rind removed
30g/1oz butter
4 leeks, trimmed, washed and sliced
460g/1lb potatoes, peeled and diced
850ml/1½ pints vegetable stock
Salt and pepper
140ml/¼ pint single cream

GARNISH
1 small tender leek, washed and thinly sliced

1 Chop the bacon into small pieces. Melt the butter in a large saucepan and fry the bacon for 2-3 minutes.
2 Add the leeks and fry for 5 minutes or until just softened.
3 Add the potatoes, stock and seasoning, bring to the boil, then reduce the heat and simmer for 45 minutes.
4 Purée in a food processor or liquidiser, then return to the rinsed out pan. Stir in the cream and reheat gently without boiling. Serve garnished with a scattering of raw sliced leeks.

Cook's Notes

Time
Preparation takes 20 minutes and cooking takes about 50 minutes.

Variation
The cream may be omitted for a less rich version of this soup.

LONDON PARTICULAR (PEA SOUP)

*In his novel Bleak House, Dickens referred to the thick fog
that often engulfed London at the time as a 'London Particular'.
As the fogs were also often called pea soupers the
names have become interchangeable.*

SERVES 8

INGREDIENTS

460g/1lb dried peas
3 rashers streaky bacon, rind removed
1 large onion, chopped
2.3litres/4 pints vegetable stock
Salt and pepper
1 tsp Worcestershire sauce

1 Soak the peas in cold water overnight, then drain.
2 Chop the bacon, place in a large saucepan and cook over a low heat until the fat begins to run. Add the onion and cook until softened.

3 Add the peas, stock, salt and pepper and bring to the boil. Reduce the heat and simmer gently for 2 hours, or until the peas are soft and mushy.
4 Purée the soup in a food processor or liquidiser. Return to the rinsed out pan. Add the Worcestershire sauce and adjust seasoning to taste. Reheat before serving.

Cook's Notes

Time
Preparation takes 10 minutes plus overnight soaking. Cooking takes about 2½ hours.

Serving Idea
Accompany with crusty bread. A little cream may be added to the soup before serving or swirled on top as a garnish.

WELSH RAREBIT

Originally called Welsh Rabbit, this snack dish became known as Welsh Rarebit in the late 18th century.

<u>SERVES 4</u>

INGREDIENTS

225g/8oz Cheddar cheese, grated
30g/1oz butter
60ml/4 tbsps beer
2 tsps dry mustard powder
Pinch of cayenne pepper
Pinch of salt
4 slices bread, toasted

1 Place the cheese, butter and beer in a small saucepan and melt over a very low heat, stirring constantly.
2 Add the mustard, cayenne and salt to taste and mix well.
3 Butter the toast well and divide the cheese mixture between the slices. Brown under a preheated grill and serve immediately.

ANGELS ON HORSEBACK

Native oysters, available only in the months with an 'r' in them, are considered by many to be the finest in the world.

<u>MAKES 12</u>

INGREDIENTS

12 fingers of bread
Butter
Juice of 1 lemon
Pinch of salt
Few drops of Tabasco sauce
12 oysters, on the half shell
12 rashers streaky bacon, rind removed

1 Toast the bread fingers, and butter them well. Keep warm on a serving plate.
2 Combine the lemon juice, salt and Tabasco in a small bowl. Remove the oysters from their shells and dip in the lemon juice mixture. Wrap a rasher of bacon around each oyster and secure with a cocktail stick.
3 Cook under a grill for 3-4 minutes turning often, until the bacon is crisp. Serve on the warm toast.

Cook's Notes

Time
For the Welsh Rarebit: preparation takes 10 minutes and cooking takes 10 minutes.

For the Angels on Horseback: preparation takes 10 minutes and cooking takes 3-4 minutes.

Variation
For Welsh Rarebit: place a slice of ham or cold roast beef on the toast before topping with the cheese.

For Angels on Horseback: substitute pieces of chicken livers or pitted prunes stuffed with chopped anchovies to create Devils on Horseback.

MUSSELS IN WHITE WINE

*The traditional French mussel stews inspired
the British, way back in Medieval days, to invent
their own versions of these delicious dishes.*

SERVES 3-4

INGREDIENTS

1.8kg/4lbs live mussels
1 large onion, finely chopped
½ bottle dry white wine
2 tsps plain flour
15g/½oz butter
Salt and pepper
Pinch of ground nutmeg
2 tbsps parsley, chopped

1 Wash and scrub the mussels well, removing the beards and discarding any that are open and will not shut when tapped lightly.
2 Place in a large saucepan, add the onion and wine. Cover and bring to the boil.

3 Cook for about 5 minutes, shaking the saucepan from time to time, or until all the mussels are open. Discard any that do not open.
4 Strain the cooking liquid into another saucepan. Remove the top shells from the mussels and put into warmed soup plates; keep warm.
5 Work the flour into the butter to make a thick paste. Add the paste in small pieces to the strained liquor, whisking it in well. Bring to the boil, stirring constantly as it thickens.
6 Season to taste with salt, pepper and nutmeg. Add the parsley and pour over the mussels.

Cook's Notes

Time
Preparation takes about 25 minutes and cooking takes 6-8 minutes.

Serving Idea
Serve with chunks of crusty bread.

SPICED POTTED MEAT

This recipe could also be called devilled potted meat because of the spices added to it. 'Devilled' dishes were very popular in Georgian times and usually included cayenne pepper and Worcestershire sauce.

SERVES 4

INGREDIENTS

460g/1lb cooked beef, pork or veal
570ml/1 pint water
¼ tsp cinnamon
¼ tsp nutmeg
¼ tsp ginger
1½ tbsps thyme
1 tbsp Worcestershire sauce
Salt and pepper
Pinch of cayenne pepper
1 tbsp chopped parsley
340g/12oz butter
Small bay leaves

1 Cut the meat into large cubes and put in a saucepan with the stock. Bring to the boil then cover and simmer until the meat is tender and almost falling apart.

2 Drain the meat and mash well with a fork. Beat in the spices, thyme, Worcestershire sauce, salt and pepper, cayenne and parsley. Spoon the mixture into small ramekins and chill.

3 Melt the butter in a saucepan over a low heat. Remove from the heat and set aside until the solids sink to the bottom and the oil rises to the top.

4 Pour into a bowl through a sieve lined with a double thickness of fine scalded muslin.

5 Spoon a layer of clarified butter over the surface of the potted meats. Chill until set.

6 Garnish with bay leaves, then add a little more clarified butter to completely cover the meat. Chill until ready to serve.

Cook's Notes

Time
Preparation takes 20 minutes and cooking takes about 1 hour.

Variation
Add a few drops of anchovy essence to the mixture before potting.

Serving Idea
Serve with toast as a snack or as a starter.

SMOKED MACKEREL PÂTÉ

*At one time, the aspic used in this recipe would
have to be made by boiling a pig's trotter in
water to extract the gelatine from it!*

<u>SERVES 4</u>

INGREDIENTS

225g/8oz smoked mackerel fillets, skin and bones removed
60g/2oz butter
Juice of ½ orange
1 tsp white wine vinegar
Salt and freshly ground black pepper
280ml/½ pint clear vegetable stock
2 tsps powdered gelatine
2 tbsps dry sherry
3 tbsps cold water

1 Put the mackerel, butter, orange juice, vinegar and seasonings into a bowl and mash with a fork.

2 Put the pâté into a serving dish and smooth the top.
3 Bring the stock to the boil in a small saucepan. Remove from the heat and cool for 1 minute.
4 Sprinkle the gelatine over and allow to stand, stirring occasionally until it has completely dissolved.
5 When the gelatine has dissolved, the liquid should be clear. At this point stir in the sherry and cold water.
6 Very carefully spoon the aspic over the top of the mackerel pâté.
7 Chill the pâté in a refrigerator until the aspic has completely set.

Cook's Notes

Time
Preparation takes about 30 minutes, plus chilling time. Cooking takes about 2 minutes.

Variation
Substitute other smoked fish, such as salmon or trout, in place of the mackerel in this recipe.

Serving Idea
For a more decorative, though not traditional finish, top the pâté with strips of canned pimento before pouring on the aspic. Alternatively, the pâté could be covered with clarified butter.

CHICKEN LIVER PÂTÉ

Many kinds of meat and fish used to be potted, pressed or turned into paste (pâté) as a means of short-term preservation. To keep the air out, the top of the mixture was sealed with clarified fat or butter.

<u>SERVES 4</u>

INGREDIENTS

30g/1oz butter for frying
1 small onion, finely chopped
Salt and pepper
225g/8oz chicken livers, trimmed
1 tsp Worcestershire sauce
60g/2oz butter, creamed
1 tbsp brandy

1 Heat the butter in a frying pan and add the onion, salt and pepper. Fry gently until the onion has softened, but not coloured.

2 Increase the heat and stir in the chicken livers. Sauté for about 2 minutes on each side, stirring continuously until just cooked through.
3 Add the Worcestershire sauce and stir.
4 Put the contents of the frying pan into a food processor or liquidiser, and blend for ½-1 minute until just smooth.
5 Add the creamed butter and the brandy and process again until the pâté is smooth.
6 Transfer the pâté to one large dish or four individual serving dishes, and refrigerate until required.

Cook's Notes

Time
Preparation takes about 15 minutes and cooking a further 15 minutes.

Cook's Tip
This pâté can be prepared in advance, but if you are not eating it straight away, seal the surface with clarified butter and refrigerate until required.

Serving Idea
Serve with toast or crusty brown bread.

PRAWN COCKTAIL

*This long established favourite starter in many restaurants
was traditionally made with scampi (Dublin Bay prawns). Ordinary prawns are now
used more often, but ensure they are fresh rather than frozen.*

<u>SERVES 4</u>

INGREDIENTS

5-6 lettuce leaves
340g/12oz cooked, peeled prawns
A little chopped parsley
4 lemon wedges, for garnish

COCKTAIL SAUCE

2 tbsps tomato purée
1 tsp Worcestershire sauce
2 tsps lemon juice
4 tsps medium sherry
60ml/4 tbsps mayonnaise
2 tbsps whipped cream

1 To make the sauce, add the tomato purée, Worcestershire sauce, lemon juice and sherry to the mayonnaise and mix well. Fold in the whipped cream.
2 Shred the lettuce finely and divide among four glass dishes. Place equal amounts of the prawns on top of the lettuce.
3 Just before serving, coat the prawns with the cocktail sauce and sprinkle a pinch of the chopped parsley on top of each glass. Accompany with lemon wedges.

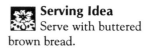

Cook's Notes

Time
Preparation takes 10 minutes.

Serving Idea
Serve with buttered brown bread.

CHAPTER TWO

FISH & SEAFOOD

FISH AND CHIPS

*This favourite national dish was established in the 1860s.
Fried fish had been sold previously to this, but its
combination with chips – thought to have been brought to these
shores from Belgium – proved to be a much bigger success.*

SERVES 4

INGREDIENTS

90g/3oz plain flour
7g/¼oz sachet easy-blend dried yeast
Pinch of sugar
75ml/2½ fl oz warm milk
75ml/2½ fl oz warm water
900g/2lbs potatoes
Oil for deep-frying
4 haddock or cod fillets, skinned
Seasoned flour

1 Place the plain flour in a mixing bowl and stir in the yeast and sugar. Gradually stir in the milk and water until a smooth batter is produced. Allow to stand for 45 minutes.

2 Peel the potatoes, rinse and dry well then cut lengthways into chips. Heat the oil in a deep-fat fryer to 180°C/350°F. Fry the chips in batches for 6-7 minutes until just tender. Drain. Bring the oil up to 190°C/375°F.

3 Dust the fish with seasoned flour and dip into the prepared batter, until well coated. Fry the fish two at a time for about 6-8 minutes, or until golden and cooked through, drain and keep warm.

4 Bring the oil back up to temperature. Fry the chips in two batches for 2-3 minutes or until golden and crisp. Serve immediately with the fish.

Cook's Notes

Time
Preparation takes 30 minutes plus 45 minutes standing time for the batter. Cooking takes about 30 minutes.

Buying Guide
Waxy potatoes are the best variety to use for chips.

SALMON FLAN

*Salmon makes a delicious filling for a flan.
This one is particularly good for picnics,
buffets or packed lunches.*

SERVES 4-6

INGREDIENTS

175g/6oz puff pastry
2 tsps cornflour
140ml/¼ pint milk
Salt and pepper
1 egg, lightly beaten
175g/6oz cooked fresh salmon

---

1 Roll the pastry out into a circle or square large enough to line a greased 20cm/8-inch flan dish. Trim off the excess pastry and crimp the edges.
2 Mix the cornflour with 1 tbsp of the milk, bring the rest nearly to the boil, then pour into the cornflour mixture. Stir well and return to the pan.

3 Bring to the boil and cook for 1 minute, stirring constantly. Season well with salt and pepper and add 15g/½oz butter.
4 Remove the pan from the heat and add the egg, beating it in thoroughly.
5 Flake the salmon, removing any bones and skin, fold it into the sauce and turn into the pastry case.
6 Bake in an oven preheated to 190°C/375°F/Gas Mark 5 for 35-40 minutes, or until golden and firm.

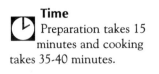

Cook's Notes

Time
Preparation takes 15 minutes and cooking takes 35-40 minutes.

Variation
Canned salmon or other fresh or canned fish can be used instead of fresh salmon.

GRILLED TROUT WITH ALMONDS

Trout is one of the most delicious of freshwater fish and lends itself to a variety of cooking methods.

SERVES 4

INGREDIENTS

1 lemon, quartered
4 fresh trout, cleaned
Salt and freshly ground black pepper
60g/2oz butter
30g/1oz flaked almonds
Parsley and lemon slices, for garnish

1 Place a lemon wedge in the cavity of each trout and season them well.
2 Line a grill pan with buttered foil and carefully lay the fish on it. Smear a little butter on each.

3 Preheat the grill to a medium heat and cook the trout under it for about 5 minutes.
4 Turn them over very carefully, put a little more butter on top and grill for another 5 minutes.
5 Keep the fish warm on serving plates while you toss the almonds in the butter in the grill pan and brown them. Ensure they do not burn.
6 Sprinkle the almonds over the fish. Serve with a garnish of lemon slices and parsley.

Cook's Notes

Time
Preparation takes 5 minutes and cooking takes 5 minutes.

Cook's Tip
The fish is cooked when the flesh flakes easily.

Buying Guide
Always buy trout with their heads on; the brightness of the eyes is a good indication of its freshness and also during cooking the eyes turn white – a sign that the fish is more or less cooked.

KEDGEREE

This dish was brought to Britain from India in the days of the Raj. Once part of the lavish traditional breakfast of country houses, Kedgeree is now more often served as a lunch or supper dish.

<u>SERVES 4</u>

INGREDIENTS

460g/1lb smoked haddock
A few peppercorns
1 bay leaf
60g/2oz butter
1 onion, chopped
175g/6oz rice
½ tsp curry powder
Juice of ½ lemon
Salt and pepper
1 tbsp chopped parsley
4 hard-boiled eggs, shelled and sliced or quartered

---

1 Put the haddock in a shallow pan with the peppercorns and bay leaf. Cover with water, bring to the boil then simmer for about 10 minutes or until the fish is tender.

2 Drain and reserve the cooking liquid. Remove the skin and bones from the fish then flake it.

3 Melt the butter in a large pan and add the onion. Fry for about 5 minutes or until softened then add the rice and cook until transparent.

4 Add the curry powder, stir well and cook gently for 1-2 minutes.

5 Measure the reserved stock and make up to 570ml/ 1 pint with water if necessary.

6 Add to the pan and bring to the boil. Stir well, cover the pan and simmer for about 20 minutes or until tender. Add more liquid if necessary.

7 When the rice is cooked, stir in the lemon juice, seasoning and haddock. Heat through, adding a little butter to moisten the mixture if necessary.

8 Turn the kedgeree onto a warm serving dish, sprinkle with the parsley and garnish with the hard-boiled eggs.

Cook's Notes

Time
Preparation takes about 15 minutes and cooking takes about 25 minutes.

Variation
Stir some cream into the dish before adding the fish. The eggs may be stirred into the rice instead of being used as a garnish.

DRESSED CRAB

*A long-time favourite in
coastal areas, where crab can
be enjoyed at its freshest.*

<u>SERVES 1-2</u>

INGREDIENTS

*1 large cooked crab
Lemon juice
Salt and pepper
Chopped parsley*

1 Pull off the crab claws and crack these with a small hammer or nutcrackers. Pull out the meat and put into a basin.

2 Turn the crab onto its back and pull the underbody firmly away from the main shell.

3 Remove and discard the stomach bag and grey feathered gills, or fingers, as these must not be eaten.

Scoop out the brown meat from the shell with a spoon and put into a second basin.

4 Cut the body in two and remove all the white meat using a skewer. Put into the first basin.

5 Carefully crack away the edge of the main shell, trimming it back to the dark line running round the edge of the shell. Use a heavy knife handle or the end of a rolling pin to crack the shell away. Scrub the shell thoroughly and rinse out.

6 Chop the white meat and season to taste with a little lemon juice, salt and pepper. Arrange the brown meat in the centre of the shell then divide the white meat and fill in the spaces on either side. Garnish with a little chopped parsley.

Cook's Notes

Time
Preparation takes about 35-45 minutes.

Variation
Garnish with hard-boiled eggs. Use 2 eggs and chop the whites finely and sieve the yolks. Arrange them in stripes on top of the crabmeat.

Peppered Mackerel with Gooseberry Sauce

The combination of gooseberries and mackerel is one which can be traced as far back as the 1700s. A popular dish in the West Country, where mackerel were plentiful, the tartness of the gooseberries is the perfect partner for the oily flesh of this fish.

SERVES 4

INGREDIENTS

4 x 225g/8oz mackerel fillets
Seasoned flour
Oil
2 tsps peppercorns, crushed

MARINADE

3 tbsps oil
Grated rind and juice of 1 lemon
1 tbsp wine vinegar
1 tbsp sugar

GOOSEBERRY SAUCE

225g/8oz gooseberries, topped and tailed
1 apple, peeled, cored and diced
60g/2oz sugar
Sprig of mint
140ml/¼ pint water
Pinch of salt
15g/½oz arrowroot mixed with a little water (optional)

1 Mix all the marinade ingredients together, pour over the fish in a shallow dish and leave to marinate for 15 minutes.

2 To make the sauce, place the gooseberries in a saucepan with the diced apple, sugar, mint and the water.

3 Bring to the boil and cook for about 8 minutes, then remove from the heat. Discard the mint and work the mixture through a sieve or purée in a blender.

4 Add a pinch of salt and return the mixture to the pan. Thicken with the arrowroot mixture, if wished and keep warm.

5 Drain the mackerel and dry on kitchen paper. Dip the fillets into seasoned flour then brush with a little oil.

6 Place on a greased grill rack and cook under a preheated grill for about 3 minutes on each side, then remove and sprinkle with the crushed peppercorns. Serve with the gooseberry sauce.

Cook's Notes

Time
Preparation takes 20 minutes and cooking takes 15 minutes.

Serving Idea
Serve with new potatoes and mushrooms.

GARNISHED POACHED SALMON

*Salmon has graced our tables for centuries and is still
considered a delicacy today, whether it is served fresh or smoked.
Wild salmon is said to have a better flavour than the farmed variety,
but both live up to the old nickname 'the king of fish'.*

SERVES 8-10

INGREDIENTS

1 fresh whole salmon, 1.15kg/2½ lbs approx, cleaned, with head
    and tail removed
1 tbsp vinegar
1 large lettuce
5-6 hard-boiled eggs
1 lemon, sliced
1 cucumber
3-4 firm tomatoes

1 Cut the fish in two crosswise. Place each section on
well-buttered pieces of foil and make two parcels,
folding over all the edges several times.

2 Place the two parcels in a saucepan large enough to
hold them side by side, cover them with cold water and
weight the parcels down with a small plate or saucer.
Add the vinegar and bring slowly to the boil. Gently
turn the parcels over in the water and then weight
them down again so they are fully immersed in the hot
water. Turn off the heat, cover the pot and leave aside
to cool.

3 Before the fish is completely cold, put the parcels on
a large plate, unwrap them and carefully remove the
skin. Lift off the top fillets and remove the bones from
the centre of the fish. Divide each section into serving-
size pieces.

4 Lay the salmon portions in two rows, the length of
one or two serving platters, with lettuce leaves between
them. Slice the hard-boiled eggs and arrange slices
overlapping.

5 Allow a slice of lemon for each salmon portion and
place accordingly. Slice the cucumber and tomatoes
and arrange together on the platter.

Cook's Notes

Time
Preparation takes 25
minutes plus cooking time.
Cooking takes about 10-15
minutes.

Serving Idea
Serve with thinly
sliced buttered bread.

PLAICE AND MUSHROOM TURNOVERS

*These delicious individual pies, evolved from the pasty,
make a warming family lunch or supper dish.*

<u>SERVES 4</u>

INGREDIENTS

4 plaice fillets, skinned
Salt and pepper
120ml/4 fl oz milk
120g/4oz button mushrooms, trimmed and thinly sliced
30g/1oz butter
Juice 1 lemon
3 tbsps breadcrumbs
340g/12oz puff pastry
Beaten egg, for glazing

---

1 Season the plaice fillets and roll them up swiss roll fashion, then secure each roll with a wooden cocktail stick.

2 Put the fish rolls in an ovenproof dish, pour over the milk and poach the fish gently for about 10 minutes in an oven preheated to 180°C/350°F/Gas Mark 4.

3 Drain the fish and allow it to cool. Remove the cocktail sticks. Increase the oven temperature to 200°C/400°F/Gas Mark 6.

4 Put the mushrooms and butter in a pan with the lemon juice. Cook over a moderate heat for about 5 minutes.

5 Allow the mushrooms to cool and then stir in the breadcrumbs.

6 Roll out the pastry, quite thinly, into 4 circles, each 15cm/6 inches in diameter. Brush the edges with beaten egg.

7 Put a fish roll into the centre of each pastry circle and top with a quarter of the mushroom mixture. Pull the pastry edges up and over the fish and pinch together to seal.

8 Place the turnovers on a greased baking sheet and glaze with the beaten egg.

9 Bake in the the reset oven for about 25 minutes, or until well risen, puffed and golden. Serve piping hot.

Cook's Notes

Time
Preparation will take about 25 minutes, plus the cooling time. Cooking will take about 35 minutes.

Serving Idea
Serve with new or mashed potatoes and a salad or green vegetable.

BAKED STUFFED MACKEREL

Mackerel is an oily fish, best suited to baking or grilling.
Stuffing the fish helps to counteract this characteristic and the addition
of herbs and oatmeal to the stuffing adds a delightful flavour.

SERVES 4

INGREDIENTS

30g/1oz butter
1 small onion, finely chopped
1 tbsp oatmeal
120g/4oz breadcrumbs
1 heaped tsp freshly chopped thyme or ½ tsp dried
1 heaped tsp freshly chopped parsley or ½ tsp dried
Salt and pepper
2-3 tbsps hot water
4 mackerel, well cleaned and washed
1 lemon, for garnish
Sprigs of thyme, for garnish

1 Melt the butter in a frying pan, add the onion and cook to soften.

2 Remove from the heat, add the oatmeal, breadcrumbs, herbs and seasoning. Mix well, then bind together with the hot water.
3 Fill the cavities of the fish with the stuffing and wrap each one separately in well-buttered foil.
4 Place in a roasting tin or on a baking sheet and bake in an oven preheated to 190°C/375°F/Gas Mark 5 for 20-30 minutes.
5 Open the parcels and serve the fish with the juices collected in the parcels. Garnish with lemon slices and sprigs of thyme.

Cook's Notes

Time
Preparation takes 20 minutes and cooking takes 20-30 minutes.

Preparation
The fish can be boned before stuffing: place the fish upright on a work surface, spreading the under-sides out and press down on the backbone pushing it towards the work surface. Turn the fish over and cut out the bone just below the head and above the tail.

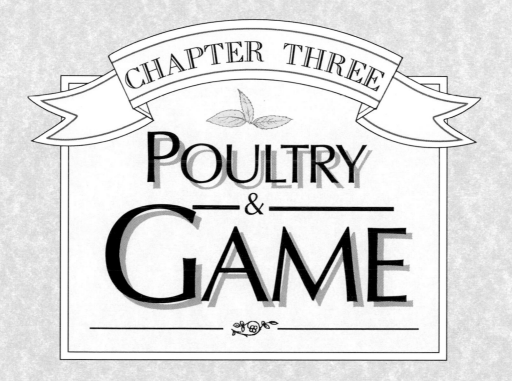

CHAPTER THREE

POULTRY
&
GAME

CHICKEN, HAM AND LEEK PIE

*The addition of cream and egg yolks at the
end of the cooking time makes this pie extra special.*

SERVES 6-8

INGREDIENTS

1 x 1.4kg/3lb chicken
1 onion
1 bay leaf
Parsley stalks
Salt and black pepper
460g/1lb leeks
30g/1oz butter
1 tbsp parsley
120g/4oz cooked ham, diced
340-400g/12-14oz puff pastry
1 large egg, lightly beaten for glazing
140ml/¼ pint double cream

1 Put the chicken in a large saucepan together with
the onion, bay leaf, parsley stalks and salt and pepper.
2 Cover with cold water and bring gently to the boil.
Allow to simmer for about 1 hour or until the chicken
is tender and the juices run clear when the thickest
part of the chicken is pierced with a skewer. Leave the
chicken to cool in the pan.
3 Meanwhile, wash and trim the leeks and cut into
4cm/1½-inch pieces. Melt the butter in a frying pan
and gently sauté the leeks for about 5 minutes. Remove
from the heat.

4 Take the cooled chicken out of the pan, remove the
skin and strip off the flesh. Cut it into good-sized
pieces. Reserve the cooking liquid.
5 Put the chicken, the ham and leeks and parsley into
a large pie dish with plenty of seasoning. Pour over
280ml/½ pint of the stock from the chicken.
6 Roll out the pastry until slightly larger than the size
of the pie dish. Use the trimmings to line the rim of the
dish. Dampen them and put on the pastry lid.
7 Trim and seal the edges together firmly. Any surplus
pastry can be used to make decorative leaves.
8 Cut a few slits in the pastry to allow the steam to
escape. Brush the pastry with some of the beaten egg.
9 Bake in the centre of an oven preheated to
230°C/450°F/Gas Mark 8, for 15 minutes then reduce
the temperature of the oven to 200°C/400°F/
Gas Mark 6 and cook the pie for another 20 minutes or
until the pastry is well risen and golden.
10 Warm the cream and remaining egg in a small pan.
When the pie is cooked remove it from the oven and
carefully lift off a segment of the pastry and stir the
warmed cream mixture into the filling.

Cook's Notes

Time
Preparation takes 1
hour for the chicken plus
cooking time. The pie
takes about 20 minutes to
prepare and 35 minutes to
bake.

Preparation
The chicken can be
cooked the day before, if
wished.

Serving Idea
Serve with a
selection of fresh
vegetables and creamed
potatoes.

BOILED CHICKEN WITH PARSLEY SAUCE

*This tasty dish was commonly served to the infirm
in Victorian days as it was palatable and easy to digest.*

SERVES 4-6

INGREDIENTS

*1 large boiling fowl or large roasting chicken about 1.8kg/4lbs
Salt and pepper
60-90g/2-3oz chicken fat
1 onion, chopped
1 carrot, chopped
1 turnip, chopped
1 stick celery, chopped
A bouquet garni*

PARSLEY SAUCE
*60g/2oz butter
60g/2oz plain flour
280ml/½ pint milk
30g/1oz chopped fresh parsley
Salt and pepper*

1 Wash and dry the bird, inside and out, and season well with salt and pepper.

2 Melt the fat in a large, deep saucepan and add the vegetables. Turn them in the fat for a few minutes then add the chicken and just enough cold water to cover the chicken.

3 Add salt and pepper and the bouquet garni. Bring to the boil, skim, then tightly cover the pan and simmer slowly for 2-2½ hours or until the chicken is tender.

4 When the bird is cooked, remove it from the pot and keep hot on a serving dish. Strain the stock from the pan and reserve it.

5 To make the sauce, melt the butter in a saucepan, stir in the flour and cook for 1 minute. Remove from the heat and gradually stir in 280ml/½ pint of the strained chicken stock.

6 Return to the heat and, when it has thickened, gradually add the milk and continue cooking until it boils again.

7 Lower the heat, cook for another 2 minutes and then remove from the heat. Add the parsley and season with salt and pepper. Serve separately in a sauce boat.

Cook's Notes

Time
Preparation takes 15 minutes and cooking takes 2-2½ hours.

Variation
The chicken may be stuffed before cooking and sewn up with a trussing needle and thread.

Cook's Tip
The chicken is cooked when a skewer inserted into the thickest part of the leg produces clear juices.

ROAST STUFFED CHICKEN

Chicken is the one meat that has been enjoyed by all sections of the population since the Middle Ages. Chickens were kept mainly for their eggs, but obviously when a bird became too old to lay eggs, it was pot roasted or stewed. Roast chicken was not as common because it required a young, tender bird.

SERVES 6

INGREDIENTS

1 small onion, finely chopped
90g/3oz fresh white breadcrumbs
Grated rind and juice of 1 lemon
1 tbsp mixed chopped fresh parsley and thyme
Salt and pepper
1 egg, beaten
Milk, if necessary
1 x 1.6kg/3½lb chicken
Melted butter

1 Make the stuffing mixture by combining the onion, breadcrumbs, lemon rind and juice, herbs, seasoning and the egg. If the mixture seems too dry add some milk.

2 Stuff the chicken at the neck end; do not pack it in too tightly. Secure the neck flap underneath the bird using a skewer. Plump up the breast.

3 Place the chicken on a trivet in a roasting tin and brush all over with some melted butter. Cover with foil and cook in an oven preheated to 180°C/350°F/Gas Mark 4, for about 1¾ hours, or until the juices run clear when the thickest part of the leg is pierced with a skewer.

4 About 30 minutes before the end of cooking, take the chicken out of the oven and remove the foil. Baste the bird with the pan juices and return to the oven to brown.

Cook's Notes

Time
Preparation takes about 20 minutes and cooking takes about 1¾ hours.

Cook's Tip
Leave the cooked chicken to stand for 10-15 minutes before carving it.

Serving Idea
Serve with bread sauce, roast potatoes and a selection of fresh vegetables.

PARTRIDGE CASSEROLE

Partridge was once a game bird reserved for the gentry.
It was turned into many a tasty dish, and was stuffed,
roasted in vine leaves and even cooked in savoury puddings.

<u>SERVES 2</u>

INGREDIENTS

30g/1oz lard
120g/4oz bacon, cubed
2 young partridges, halved
Seasoned flour
1 small onion, chopped
1 carrot, sliced
2 sticks celery, sliced
1 cooking apple, peeled, cored and sliced
15g/½oz flour
175ml/6 fl oz dry white wine or cider
175ml/6 fl oz game stock
2 parsley stalks
1 sprig thyme
1 sprig marjoram
Salt and black pepper
90g/3oz seedless raisins
140ml/¼ pint single cream

1 Heat the lard in a heavy-based casserole and add the bacon. Fry gently until brown and remove.

2 Dust the partridge halves with seasoned flour and fry until well browned on all sides. Remove from the dish.
3 Add the vegetables and apple slices to the casserole and fry for 5 minutes. Add the flour and stir for a minute before adding the wine or cider, stock, herbs, seasoning and raisins.
4 Return the partridges to the casserole. Cover with a lid and cook slowly for 25-30 minutes, or until the meat is tender.
5 Remove the partridge halves to a hot serving dish and keep warm.
6 If the sauce is too runny, boil to reduce slightly. Lower the heat and add the cream, do not allow the sauce to boil again. Adjust the seasoning, discard the herbs and pour the sauce over the partridges.

Cook's Notes

Time
Preparation takes 20 minutes and cooking takes about 40 minutes.

Serving Idea
Accompany with triangles of bread fried in oil. Serve with carrots, peas and potatoes.

RABBIT IN MUSTARD SAUCE

Rabbit was first brought to Britain by the Romans who were very partial to its flavour. Later it became a very popular cheap source of meat for the British and quite a number of imaginative recipes were invented to suit its delicate flavour.

SERVES 4

INGREDIENTS

1 x 1.8kg/4lb rabbit, cleaned and cut into serving pieces
60ml/4 tbsps mild mustard
30g/1oz butter
15g/½oz dripping
1 medium onion, finely chopped
30g/1oz plain flour
2 sprigs fresh thyme or ¾ tsp dried
1 sprig fresh rosemary or ¾ tsp dried
420ml/¾ pint dry cider or white wine
Salt and freshly ground black pepper

1 Smear the rabbit pieces with the mustard and set aside for a couple of hours to absorb the flavour.

2 Melt the butter and dripping together in a large frying pan and when the foam subsides fry the rabbit pieces, a few at a time, until golden brown. Transfer them to a flameproof casserole.

3 Add the chopped onion to the frying pan, adding a little more fat if necessary. Fry until soft and then add the flour and herbs, stirring constantly.

4 Cook for 1-2 minutes over a gentle heat, then add the cider. Stir the sauce well and bring to the boil.

5 Season to taste and pour the thickened sauce over the rabbit pieces. Cover the casserole and simmer gently for 45 minutes-1 hour, or until tender.

Cook's Notes

Time
Preparation takes 20 minutes plus 2-3 hours marinating. Cooking takes about 1 hour.

Serving Idea
Accompany with new potatoes and a green vegetable or a green salad.

Variation
The sauce ingredients will taste equally good with chicken portions or pork chops.

PHEASANTS IN RED WINE

*This ancient method of cooking pheasant is ideal
for birds in their second season which
need longer, slower cooking than young ones.*

<u>SERVES 4</u>

INGREDIENTS

45g/1½oz butter
2 prepared pheasants
2 eating apples, quartered or chopped
1 onion
2 tbsps plain flour
280ml/½ pint game or chicken stock
140ml/¼ pint red wine
Grated rind and juice of 1 orange
1 heaped tsp brown sugar
Salt and pepper
Bay leaf, sprig of parsley and thyme, tied together

1 Melt the butter in a large heavy pan. Add the pheasants one at a time, turning to brown all over. Remove and place in a casserole dish with the apples.

2 Chop the onion and add it to the fat in the pan. Allow it to soften without browning.

3 Stir in the flour, gradually add the stock and the wine and bring to the boil, stirring constantly.

4 Add the grated orange rind and juice, and the sugar. Season with salt and pepper then pour the sauce over the pheasant.

5 Add the herbs, cover the casserole and bake in an oven preheated to 180°C/350°F/Gas Mark 4, for 1¼-1½ hours or until tender.

Cook's Notes

Time
Preparation takes 15 minutes and cooking takes 1¼-1½ hours.

Buying Guide
Hen pheasants tend to be more tender than cock pheasants.

ROAST SADDLE OF VENISON WITH SPICED PEARS

Once mainly eaten by nobility and gentle folk, today's farming methods mean venison is more widely available, although the price ensures it is still reserved for special occasions.

<u>SERVES 8-10</u>

MARINADE
280ml/½ pint good oil
280ml/½ pint red wine vinegar
570ml/1 pint red wine
Bouquet garni
A few parsley stalks
Rind of ½ orange
8 juniper berries, crushed
1 sliced onion
1 stick celery
1 clove garlic, crushed

1 saddle venison, weighing 2.8-3.25kg/6-7lbs
Butter
Salt and pepper
4-5 ripe pears (allow half a pear per diner)
2 tsps cinnamon

1 Bring all the marinade ingredients to the boil in a saucepan. Simmer for 5 minutes then leave to cool.
2 Place the venison in a large dish and pour over the marinade to cover. Leave in a cool place for 2 days, turning the meat several times during marinating.
3 Remove the venison from the marinade and pat dry with kitchen paper. Lay the meat in a large roasting tin, rub the surface with butter and sprinkle with salt and pepper.
4 Cover with foil and roast in an oven preheated to 190°C/375°F/Gas Mark 5, for about 1½-2 hours, basting the meat frequently. Cooking time depends on taste – for rare meat cook for 10-15 minutes per 500g/1lb and for medium done meat cook for 13-18 minutes per 500g/1lb.
5 About 30 minutes before end of cooking time, peel and slice the pears in half, dot them with butter and sprinkle with cinnamon. Add to the roasting tin and baste together with the meat.
6 Remove the foil 10 minutes before the end of cooking and raise the temperature to 200°C/400°F/Gas Mark 6, to brown the meat and pears.
7 Remove the meat and pears from the tin and keep warm on a serving dish while making gravy with the pan juices.
8 To carve the venison, cut down either side of the central backbone then cut long slices from the length of the joint.

Cook's Notes

Time
Preparation takes about 30 minutes plus 2 days marinating. Cooking time takes 1½-2 hours.

Cook's Tip
Venison is usually served rare and the juices should run pink from the meat.

Buying Guide
Serve with redcurrant jelly and game chips (see Roast Pheasant recipe).

JUGGED HARE

As its name suggests, this recipe was originally cooked in a tall jug set in a pan of water. The sauce was traditionally thickened with the hares blood to make a lovely rich sauce, but this is optional.

SERVES 4

INGREDIENTS

90g/3oz dripping
1 onion, sliced
1 carrot, sliced
1 turnip, sliced
1 hare, jointed, with its blood (optional)
Seasoned flour
280ml/½ pint game stock
140ml/¼ pint red wine
2 sprigs parsley
2 sprigs thyme
1 sprig marjoram
4 cloves
4 allspice berries
Grated rind of 1 lemon
Salt and pepper

1 Heat half the dripping in a heavy-based casserole and fry the vegetables for 2-3 minutes. Remove from the dish and add the remaining fat.

2 Coat the joints of meat in seasoned flour, add to the casserole, in batches if necessary, and fry to brown all over.

3 Return the vegetables to the casserole and stir in the stock and wine. Add all the herbs, spices, lemon rind and seasoning.

4 Bring to the boil, then cover and cook in an oven preheated to 160°C/325°F/Gas Mark 3, for about 3 hours or until the hare is tender. (To cook the hare in the traditional manner, put the ingredients into a large heatproof jug or basin instead of the casserole. Seal the top with greaseproof paper and foil. Stand the vessel in a large, deep saucepan and add enough boiling water to come about two-thirds of the way up the sides of the jug or basin. Cover the pan and simmer over a low heat for 3½-4 hours, topping up the water level with more boiling water whenever necessary.)

5 If using the hares blood to thicken the dish, remove the meat and vegetables from the casserole and keep warm.

6 Melt 15g/½oz butter in a saucepan and stir in 1 tbsp flour. Gradually add the cooking juices and the hare's blood, cook until thickened and pour over the hare. Do not allow to boil.

7 Alternatively, knead together about 15g/½oz butter and 2 tbsps flour to form a paste. Whisk into the hot juices in small pieces until the sauce thickens. Serve immediately.

Cook's Notes

Time
Preparation takes 30 minutes and cooking takes about 3 hours.

Serving Idea
Accompany with redcurrant jelly and serve with green vegetables, creamed potatoes and carrots.

Buying Guide
If you want to use the hares blood to thicken the sauce, you will need to buy the hare from a good butcher who will supply the blood with it.

ROAST PHEASANT

*Pheasant, one of our most popular game birds, is in
season from the beginning of October to the end of January.*

SERVES 4

INGREDIENTS
*2 young hen pheasants, cleaned
4 rashers of streaky bacon
Softened butter
140ml/¼ pint stock
140ml/¼ pint red wine or port
2 tbsps redcurrant jelly
30g/1oz fine breadcrumbs
Watercress, to garnish*

STUFFING
*45g/1½oz butter
1 small onion, finely chopped
1 cooking apple
Juice of ½ lemon
Salt and black pepper*

GAME CHIPS
*3-4 medium potatoes
Oil for deep-frying
Salt*

1 To make the stuffing, heat 15g/½oz of the butter in a
small pan, add the chopped onion and cook until soft
and transparent.

2 Grate the apple into a bowl and quickly sprinkle
with the lemon juice. Add the onion together with the
remaining butter, softened. Season to taste and mix all
the ingredients together well.

3 Divide the stuffing between the cavities of the
cleaned pheasants packing it well in. Sew up the
cavities with a trussing needle and fine string.

4 Sprinkle the birds with freshly ground black pepper
and cover the breast with the bacon. Spread with some
softened butter all over the birds before placing them in
a roasting tin.

5 Roast the pheasants in an oven preheated to
190°C/375°F/Gas Mark 5, for about 1 hour, basting
every 15 minutes. Test with a skewer in the thickest
part of the leg, when the juices run slightly pink or
clear (depending on taste) remove the pheasants from
the oven – do not over cook or the meat will be dry
and tough. Lift the pheasants onto a carving dish,
remove the string and bacon and keep warm.

6 Skim the roasting juices to remove as much fat as
possible, then put the roasting tin over a moderate heat.

7 Add the stock and red wine or port and simmer,
stirring continually and incorporating all the browned
essence that may be stuck to the bottom of the tin.

8 Stir in the redcurrant jelly and breadcrumbs and
keep stirring until the sauce thickens slightly. Adjust
the seasoning and then transfer to a sauceboat.

9 Garnish the pheasant with sprigs of watercress before
serving with game chips.

GAME CHIPS

1 Peel and wash the potatoes, then slice thinly into
rounds. Plunge into cold water and pat dry.

2 Heat the oil in a deep-fat fryer to 196°C/385°F. Fry
the potato slices, in batches if necessary, for about 3
minutes then remove and allow the fat to regain its
original heat. Fry the chips again for just 1-2 minutes or
until golden.

3 Drain well on kitchen paper, sprinkle with salt and
serve immediately with the pheasant.

Cook's Notes

Time
Preparation time
takes 45 minutes and
cooking time takes about
1¼ hours.

Preparation
Adding stuffing to
the pheasants and
covering them with bacon
helps to keep the birds

moist, as the meat can easily
dry out during roasting.
Regular basting during
cooking is also important.

CHAPTER FOUR

MEAT

STUFFED BREAST OF LAMB

Sussex is an area which boasts fine flavoured lamb, and this recipe from the region makes good use of an inexpensive cut of lamb.

<u>SERVES 4-6</u>

INGREDIENTS

900g-1.4kg/2-3lb boned breast of lamb, bones and trimmings reserved
1 medium onion
Salt and pepper
225g/8oz fresh white breadcrumbs
30g/1oz shredded suet
½ tsp marjoram
½ tsp thyme
Grated rind and juice of ½ lemon
1 egg, lightly beaten
2-3 tbsps plain flour

1 Place the lamb bones and trimmings in a saucepan with half the onion and some salt and pepper. Cover with 570ml/1 pint water, bring to the boil and skim the surface. Cover the pan and simmer for 1 hour.
2 To make the stuffing, mix the breadcrumbs, suet, herbs, lemon rind and juice and some seasoning together in a bowl. Finely chop the remaining onion and add. Stir in the egg and 2-3 tbsps of the stock, if necessary, to bind the mixture together.
3 Spread the stuffing over the lamb and roll up, starting at the wide end. Tie firmly with string at 5cm/2-inch intervals and place in a roasting tin. Spread with a little butter and roast in an oven preheated to 200°C/400°F/Gas Mark 6, for 1½-2 hours, basting several times during cooking.
4 While the lamb is cooking, strain the stock and return to the pan. Boil rapidly to reduce to about 280ml/½ pint.
5 When the meat is cooked, transfer it to a serving dish and keep warm while you make the gravy. Drain off the excess fat from the roasting tin, retaining the browned meat juices.
6 Stir the flour into the pan and heat until the mixture starts to bubble. Gradually stir in the strained stock and bring to the boil, stirring constantly. Boil until thickened then pour into a sauce boat and serve with the lamb.

Cook's Notes

Time
Preparation takes 30 minutes. Cooking takes 1 hour for the stock and 1½-2 hours for the lamb.

Variation
Some of the breadcrumbs in the stuffing can be replaced with chopped bacon.

STEAK AND KIDNEY PIE

*This pie is definitely a national favourite, and has been
popular since the Middle Ages. Oysters would have been added
to the dish in days when they were cheap and plentiful,
but mushrooms are more common today.*

SERVES 4-6

INGREDIENTS

680g/1½ lb rump or stewing steak
175g/6oz kidney
60g/2oz butter
2 medium onions, finely chopped
2 tbsps seasoned flour
*420-570ml/¾-1 pint beef stock or stock mixed with
    some red wine*
120g/4oz mushrooms (optional)
400g/14oz packet of frozen puff pastry, defrosted
Salt and freshly milled black pepper
Beaten egg for glazing

1 Trim the steak and cut into even-sized cubes. Core
and dice the kidneys.
2 Heat some of the butter in a flameproof casserole
dish and add the onions. Cook for 5 minutes or until
soft. Remove from the pan.
3 Roll the steak in half the seasoned flour and add to
the hot butter in batches, adding more butter as
necessary. Cook until browned all over, remove from
the pan and brown the kidney in the same way.
4 Return all the meat and onions to the casserole
along with any juices that have accumulated. Sprinkle
over the plain flour and stir in well.
5 Gradually stir in the stock, bring to the boil, turn the
heat down and cover and simmer for about 1½ hours,

or until the meat is tender. Alternatively, cook in an
oven at 160°C/300°F/ Gas Mark 2 for the same amount
of time.
6 Slice the mushrooms, if using, and add to the meat
and gravy. Let the mixture cool. Spoon the meat and
mushrooms into an 850ml/1½-pint pie dish, piling it up
in the centre or inserting a pie funnel to hold the
pastry up. Add 140ml/¼ pint of the gravy.
7 On a floured work surface, roll out the pastry to at
least 2.5cm/1 inch larger than the size of the pie dish.
Use the pie dish as a guide to cut the pie lid.
8 Moisten the rim of the pie dish and cut a strip from
the edge of the pastry to cover the rim. Moisten the
pastry strip and place on the rim. Then moisten the
pastry on the rim and place the pie lid over the meat.
Seal, then trim and flute the edges.
9 Glaze the pie with the beaten egg. Decorate the top
with leaves cut from the pastry trimmings and glaze
those too.
10 Place in an oven preheated to 220°C/425°F/
Gas Mark 7, for 15 minutes, then lower the heat to
180°C/350°F/Gas Mark 4 and bake for a further 30-40
minutes or until well risen and golden brown. Serve the
rest of the gravy separately.

Cook's Notes

⏲ Time
Preparation takes
45 minutes, cooking takes
about 2½ hours.

◕ Buying Guide
Rump steak will give
the best flavour, but
stewing steak will work
well.

◣ Variation
Add oysters instead
of mushrooms just before
putting on the pie crust for
a treat.

CAWL

*This dish is one of the most popular Welsh stews and one which
has as many variations as there are Welsh cooks. Lamb, beef
or bacon or a mixture of all these meats may be used along
with a selection of fresh winter vegetables.*

<u>SERVES 8</u>

INGREDIENTS

30g/1oz lard
680g/1½lbs scrag end of lamb in one piece
2 onions, chopped
2 parsnips, peeled and cut into chunks
1 large turnip, peeled and cut into chunks
3-4 carrots, peeled and cut into thick slices
460g/1lb piece smoked bacon, cubed
Few peppercorns
1 bay leaf
1 sprig parsley
1 sprig rosemary
About 2.3 litres/4 pints light stock or water
460g/1lb potatoes, peeled and cut into chunks
4 leeks, washed and thickly sliced

1 Melt the lard in a frying pan and fry the lamb on all
sides until brown; transfer to a flameproof casserole.

2 Fry the onions, parsnips, turnip and carrots until just
beginning to soften, in batches if necessary, and add to
the meat.

3 Add the bacon, peppercorns, bay leaf, parsley and
rosemary to the casserole and add the stock or water to
cover.

4 Bring gently to the boil and skim off any scum that
rises to the surface. Reduce the heat, cover and simmer
for 2-3 hours.

5 Add the potatoes and leeks to the casserole and
cook for a further 30 minutes.

6 To serve, slice the meat, divide between the serving
bowls and then spoon over the vegetables and broth.

Cook's Notes

Time
Preparation takes 30
minutes and cooking takes
2½-3½ hours.

Cook's Tip
If wished, soak the
piece of bacon in water
overnight before using to
reduce the strong salty
flavour.

Serving Idea
Cawl is traditionally
served with a wedge of
Welsh cheese and chunks
of bread.

LIVER WITH ONIONS

*The combination of liver and onions dates back to Medieval times,
when plenty of herbs were added to the dish to disguise the
then rather strong flavour of the liver.*

SERVES 4-6

INGREDIENTS

460g/1lb onions
Salt and freshly ground black pepper
45g/1½oz plain flour
460g/1lb lambs' liver, trimmed and thinly sliced
60g/2oz butter
2 tbsps fresh chopped parsley

1 Peel the onions and slice thinly, keeping each slice in circles if possible.

2 Mix the seasoning and the flour together on a plate and lay the slices of liver into the flour, turning them and pressing them gently to coat all over evenly.
3 Put the butter into a large frying pan. Heat gently until foaming. Add the onion rings and fry until just turning golden.
4 Add the liver slices and fry for 2-3 minutes on each side – the exact cooking time will depend on the thickness of each slice.
5 Stir the parsley into the liver and onions and serve immediately on hot plates.

Cook's Notes

Time
Preparation takes 15 minutes, cooking takes about 10 minutes.

Variation
Add 120g/4oz shredded streaky bacon with the onions.

Watchpoint
Do not overcook liver or any offal, as it will toughen. Liver is best served still slightly pink in the centre.

Serving Idea
Serve with creamed potatoes and green vegetables. Accompany with lemon wedges.

BEEF BRAISED IN ALE

*This North Country dish probably started out as a
farmhouse recipe as most farmers brewed their own ale, which
often found its way into stews and casseroles as well as tankards!*

SERVES 4

INGREDIENTS

680g/1½lbs braising steak, about 2.5cm/1-inch thick
2 onions
225g/8oz carrots
2-3 tbsps plain flour
Salt and black pepper
45g/1½oz dripping
1 sprig of thyme
1 sprig of parsley
420ml/¾ pint ale
1 tsp honey

1 Cut the steak into about twelve pieces.
2 Peel the onions and chop them fairly small. Peel the carrots and cut them into pieces about the size of your little finger.
3 Put the flour on a plate and mix in 1 tsp of salt and a good sprinkling of pepper.
4 Heat the dripping in a frying pan, add the onions and cook until soft. Transfer them with a slotted spoon to a large, shallow, greased casserole.

5 Fry the carrots for 1-2 minutes then add to the onions.
6 Dip the pieces of meat in the seasoned flour and brown them in the fat in the pan.
7 Remove these as they are cooked and place in the casserole on top of the vegetables, in a single layer.
8 If necessary, add a little more dripping to the pan then stir in the remainder of the seasoned flour.
9 Cook for a minute or two, stirring all the time, then add the herbs and pour on the ale. Allow to boil for a minute or two, then add the honey and pour over the meat.
10 Cover the dish either with a lid or with foil and cook in an oven preheated to 160°C/325°F/Gas Mark 3 for 1-1½ hours, or until the meat is tender.
11 If the gravy looks as though it needs to be a little thicker, mix 1 tsp of arrowroot with 2 tbsps of cold water and stir into the gravy 15 minutes before the end of cooking. Remove the herbs before serving.

Cook's Notes

Time
Preparation takes about 20 minutes and cooking takes 1-1½ hours.

Variation
Use your favourite ale, beer or stout in this recipe.

Preparation
The cooking time will depend on the cut of beef that you use. Cheaper cuts need longer cooking than more expensive ones.

ROAST HERBED LEG OF LAMB

A delicious herb and breadcrumb coating adds
extra flavour to one of our favourite cuts of lamb.

<u>SERVES 6</u>

INGREDIENTS

1½kg/3½lb leg of lamb
2 bay leaves
120g/4oz butter
225g/8oz breadcrumbs
1 tsp chopped fresh thyme
1 tsp chopped fresh rosemary
1 tbsp chopped fresh parsley
Juice of 2 lemons
Salt and freshly ground black pepper

1 Prepare a sheet of foil large enough to wrap around the meat completely.
2 Put the meat onto the foil with the bay leaves underneath.

3 In a small bowl, mix the butter thoroughly with the remaining ingredients. Spread this mixture over the upper surface of the meat, using a wet palette knife.
4 Loosely wrap the foil around the joint of meat, place in a roasting tin and roast in an oven preheated to 200°C/400°F/Gas Mark 6, for about 1-1½ hours, depending on how pink you like your lamb.
5 About 30 minutes before the end of cooking, remove the roast from the oven, unwrap the foil and baste the joint with the melted fat that has collected in the bottom of the parcel.
6 Return the meat to the oven and continue roasting, uncovered, for a further 30 minutes until the crust is brown and crisp.

Cook's Notes

Time
Preparation takes about 15 minutes, and cooking takes about 1-1½ hours. The exact cooking time will depend on how pink you like your lamb.

Cook's Tip
The breadcrumb mixture in this recipe is also delicious when used to coat a joint of gammon.

Serving Idea
Serve with buttered new potatoes and seasonal vegetables.

PORK CHOPS WITH APPLES AND CIDER

*The combination of cider and pork is a traditional West Country association.
As cider was the region's most popular beverage it was often used in cooking
and was also commonly partnered with chicken and mackerel.*

SERVES 4

INGREDIENTS

4 pork chops
1 onion, finely chopped
½ tsp sage
½ tsp thyme
280ml/½ pint cider
45g/1½oz butter
60g/2oz flour, seasoned with salt and pepper
1 or 2 apples, peeled, cored and sliced
140ml/¼ pint light stock
1 tsp honey

1 Place the chops in a shallow ovenproof dish which is just large enough to hold them.

2 Add the onion and herbs to the cider and pour over the chops. Leave to marinate for several hours, turning the meat occasionally.

3 Heat the butter in a frying pan. Drain the chops and dust them with some of the seasoned flour, lightly coating both sides. Add them to the frying pan and seal both sides, browning them slightly.

4 Strain the marinade into a bowl. Wash and grease the baking dish. Layer the sliced apple on the bottom and place the chops on top.

5 Add the onion from the marinade to the fat in the frying pan. Cook until soft and stir in the remainder of the seasoned flour.

6 Allow it to brown, stirring constantly, then gradually stir in the liquid from the marinade and the stock. Stir in the honey, bring to the boil and pour over the chops.

7 Cover with foil and cook in an oven preheated to 180°C/350°F/Gas Mark 4, for 45 minutes or until tender.

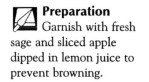

Cook's Notes

Time
Preparation takes 20 minutes plus 3-4 hours marinating time. Cooking takes about 45 minutes.

Preparation
Garnish with fresh sage and sliced apple dipped in lemon juice to prevent browning.

Variation
A few tablespoons of clotted or double cream may be stirred into the sauce just before serving.

Serving Idea
Serve with peas and creamed potatoes.

GUARD OF HONOUR WITH APRICOT STUFFING

This was a popular way of serving lamb in Edwardian days when along with the similar 'crown roast', it made an impressive and not too expensive centre-piece on many dining tables.

SERVES 6

INGREDIENTS

APRICOT STUFFING
175g/6oz dried apricots, soaked overnight
30g/1oz butter
1 small onion, finely chopped
120g/4oz fresh white breadcrumbs
60g/2oz blanched split almonds
2 tbsps chopped parsley
Salt and black pepper
Juice of ½ lemon
1-2 eggs, lightly beaten

2 even-sized best ends of neck of lamb each weighing about
  680g-900g/1½-2lbs, trimmed and chined
Seasoned flour

1 To make the stuffing, drain and chop the soaked apricots. Melt the butter in a small pan and sauté the chopped onion for 5 minutes until softened.

2 Put the apricots, breadcrumbs, almonds, parsley and salt and pepper in a large bowl.

3 Add the onion, lemon juice and enough of the beaten egg to bind the mixture together. Mix together well.

4 Stand the lamb racks up, and with the skin sides facing outwards, interlock the bones. Fill the central cavity with the stuffing mixture, making sure that it is not too tightly packed.

5 Tie pieces of string around the guard, securing between each set of bones to hold the roast together. Cover the bone ends with foil to stop them from burning during cooking.

6 Lightly dust the skin of the lamb with a little seasoned flour – this will help to crisp it.

7 Transfer the guard to a roasting tin and cook in an oven preheated to 200°C/400°F/Gas Mark 6, for 15 minutes.

8 Reduce the oven temperature to 180°C/350°F/Gas Mark 4, and cook for a further 40 minutes-1 hour, depending on how you like your lamb – test the lamb with a skewer to see how pink the juices are.

9 When the lamb is cooked, remove it from the oven and transfer to a hot serving dish. Leave to stand for 10-15 minutes before carving. Make gravy with the pan juices, and if wished add a little wine, sherry or redcurrant jelly for extra flavour. To carve the lamb, remove the string and cut down through the meat each side of the rib bones.

Cook's Notes

Time
Preparation takes 25 minutes and cooking takes 1-1¼ hours.

Cook's Tip
Before you stuff the lamb, make sure that it is at room temperature.

Buying Guide
Make sure you buy two racks that have the same number of bones, or you won't be able to fit them together evenly.

ROAST RIBS OF BEEF

A traditional favourite for Sunday lunch, especially when served with all the trimmings.

<u>SERVES 6-8</u>

INGREDIENTS

2.3kg/5lb forerib of beef on the bone
A little lard or butter
Freshly ground black pepper
2 tbsps flour
280ml/½ pint brown stock
Salt and black pepper

1 Set the joint of beef on a rack in a large roasting tin. Rub the meat with softened butter or lard, season it with black pepper and put into an oven preheated to 220°C/425°F/Gas Mark 7, for 15-20 minutes in order to sear the meat.

2 Then reduce the oven temperature to 200°C/400°F/Gas Mark 6 for 1¼-1¾ hours, depending on how well cooked you like your beef. Baste regularly.
3 Remove the meat from the oven when cooked and transfer to a hot serving dish. Allow to stand for 10-15 minutes before carving.
4 Pour the excess fat from the tin and keep it in a cup or jug. Set the pan on top of the oven or hob on a low heat. Add the flour to the browned meat juices and stir well for 3-4 minutes before adding the stock.
5 Bring to the boil, stirring continually with a wooden spoon, season to taste and simmer for 2-3 minutes. Transfer the gravy to a sauce boat.

YORKSHIRE PUDDINGS

Originally called 'dripping pudding' it was usually served as a first course with gravy to take the edge off appetites before the roast beef course.

<u>MAKES 12</u>

INGREDIENTS

120g/4oz plain flour
½ tsp salt
1 egg
280ml/½ pint milk
30g/1oz dripping (from roasting the beef)

1 In a bowl, sift together the flour and salt. Make a well in the middle and drop in the egg.
2 Gradually mix to a smooth batter using half the

milk. If time allows, leave the mixture to stand for 1 hour then beat in the rest of the milk.
3 Pour 1 tsp of the dripping into each well in a 12-space patty tin and put into an oven preheated to 220°C/425°F/Gas Mark 7, for a few minutes or until the fat is smoking.
4 Remove and pour some batter into each space so they are two-thirds full. Return the tin to the top shelf of the oven and bake for 15-20 minutes until the Yorkshire puddings are puffed up and golden brown. Serve immediately.

Cook's Notes

Time
For Roast Ribs of Beef: preparation takes 15 minutes and cooking takes 1½-2 hours.

For Yorkshire Puddings: preparation takes 15 minutes, plus 1 hour standing, cooking takes 15-20 minutes.

Serving Idea
For Roast Ribs of Beef: serve with Yorkshire Pudding, horseradish sauce or mustard.

For Yorkshire Puddings: these can also be served as a sweet course. Accompany with golden syrup or butter and sugar.

PORK PIE

This raised pie was originally made in Melton Mowbray, Leicestershire, to feed hungry riders after a hard day's hunting with the hounds.

<u>SERVES 4-6</u>

INGREDIENTS
STOCK
570ml/1 pint water
Pork or veal bones, or 1 pig's trotter
1 bay leaf
1 onion
Salt
4 peppercorns

FILLING
120g/4oz streaky bacon
680g/1½lbs pork fillet
Salt and pepper
Pinch of powdered mustard
3 fresh sage leaves, finely chopped
1 tbsp water

HOT-WATER CRUST PASTRY
340g/12oz plain flour
½ tsp salt
150g/5oz lard
140ml/¼ pint water and milk mixed half and half
Beaten egg, to glaze

1 To make the stock, place all the ingredients in a large saucepan. Cover and simmer for 2-3 hours. Strain the stock, return to the pan and boil rapidly until reduced to about 280ml/½ pint of concentrated stock. Set aside – the stock should set to a jelly when it cools.
2 To prepare the filling, finely dice the bacon and pork, then mix with the seasoning, mustard, sage and water.
3 To make the pastry, sieve the flour and salt into a warmed mixing bowl and make a well in the centre.

Heat the lard and water and milk mixture in a saucepan until boiling, then remove from the heat and pour into the well in the flour. Mix together quickly with a wooden spoon until thick, and knead by hand until smooth. If the pastry is too dry add a few drops of boiling water.
4 Cut off one third of the pastry and keep warm and moist. Mould the rest, while it is still warm, over a large warmed and floured Kilner jar, or use to line a greased and warmed raised pie mould or spring-form cake tin, about 18cm/7 inches in diameter. Mould the pastry with your knuckles and thumbs, working it up the mould. If moulding the pastry round a tin or jar, ease the finished pie case off the mould, and tie a double strip of greaseproof paper round it.
5 Stand the pie case on a baking sheet and fill it with the meat. Roll out the reserved pastry to make a lid. Dampen the top edge of the pie and firmly press on the lid, crimping the edges together to seal. Make a hole in the centre of the lid to allow the steam to escape, then brush the surface with beaten egg to glaze.
6 Bake in the centre of an oven preheated to 180°C/350°F/Gas Mark 4, for 1¾-2 hours, or until the pastry is golden brown and firm. Remove the greaseproof paper or pie mould after the pie has been cooking for 45 minutes.
7 When the pie is cooked, remove from the oven and allow to cool. Warm the jellied stock until it is just melted, then using a small funnel, pour in as much stock as the pie will hold through the centre hole in the crust. Leave to set for 1 hour in the refrigerator.

Cook's Notes

Time
Preparation takes 45 minutes and cooking takes 4-5 hours plus 1 hour refrigeration.

Variation
A filling of chicken and pork may be used instead of all pork.

Preparation
A little anchovy essence added to the filling will keep it a pale pink colour.

Baked, Glazed Gammon

One of the best areas for gammon and ham curing is Wiltshire, and a variety of recipes for cooking ham can be attributed to this county. Often served cold, or used as a tasty sandwich filling in other parts of the country, here ham was eaten hot like a Sunday roast.

Serves 4-6

Ingredients
900g-1.15kg/2-2½lbs smoked gammon
1 clove-studded onion
A few peppercorns
1 tbsp honey
3 tbsps mustard
2 tbsps soft brown sugar
Whole cloves

1 Soak the gammon in water for at least twelve hours, rinse and cover with cold water. Add the clove-studded onion, peppercorns and honey.

2 Bring slowly to the boil, skim, then simmer for 1-1½ hours or until tender.

3 Remove the ham from the water, pat dry and score the skin in a diamond pattern.

4 Mix together the mustard and sugar and spread the mixture evenly over the skin. Stud with whole cloves if wished and place in a roasting tin.

5 Bake in an oven preheated to 200°C/400°F/Gas Mark 6, for 30-40 minutes or until the glaze has browned. Cut into thick slices to serve.

Cook's Notes

Time
Preparation takes about 30 minutes plus at least 12 hours soaking time. Cooking takes 1½-2 hours.

Serving Idea
Serve with parsley sauce or a rich brown sauce and accompany with new or creamed potatoes and a green vegetable.

Variation
If wished green (unsmoked) gammon or ham can be used for this recipe and the soaking omitted.

CORNISH PASTIES

These pasties were originally made as a portable meal-in-one that could be taken by miners down the cornish tin mines. Traditional pasties were very large and made with a thick rope-like edging on one side for the miner to use as a handle, thus preventing the rest of his meal getting dirty. Initials were also marked on one corner so that if the pasty was only half eaten, it could be identified later!

<u>SERVES 6</u>

INGREDIENTS

225g/8oz plain flour
Pinch of salt
60g/2oz butter
60g/2oz lard
Cold water, to mix
225g/8oz lean steak
1 small onion, finely chopped
1 potato, peeled and cut into small dice
120g/4oz swede or turnip, peeled and cut into small dice
Salt and pepper
1 egg, beaten

1 Place the flour and salt into a mixing bowl. Rub the butter and lard into the flour until the mixture resembles fine breadcrumbs. Add enough water to mix to a firm dough. Chill until required.

2 Cut the steak into small thin strips, place in a bowl with the prepared vegetables and season to taste.

3 Roll out the dough and cut out 6 circles, using a tea plate as a guide. Divide the meat mixture into six and pile into the centre of each circle of pastry.

4 Dampen the edges with beaten egg. Fold the pastry in half so that the edges of the pastry meet on top of the filling; pinch together with fingers to seal.

5 Place on a lightly greased baking sheet and brush with beaten egg to glaze. Cut a small slit in the top of each pasty to allow the steam to escape.

6 Bake in an oven preheated to 190°C/375°F/Gas Mark 5, for 20-35 minutes, or until golden.

Cook's Notes

Time
Preparation takes 45 minutes and cooking takes 30-35 minutes.

Serving Idea
Serve hot or cold as a snack.

SHEPHERD'S PIE

Shepherd's Pie was originally devised as a way of using up leftover meat and potatoes, but the recipe has come a long way since then. It is doubtful if it ever had much to do with shepherds, but it could be a reference to the use of lamb, as opposed to Cottage Pie which is usually made with beef.

SERVES 4

INGREDIENTS

30g/1oz fat
1 onion, chopped
1 carrot, diced
460g/1lb cooked lamb, minced
Pinch of mixed herbs
Salt and pepper
280ml/½ pint brown stock
30g/1oz cornflour
900g/2lbs cooked potatoes
60g/2oz butter

1 Heat the fat in a large frying pan and add the onion and carrot. Cook for 3 minutes or until the onion is softened.

2 Add the meat and cook for 3 minutes. Stir in the herbs, seasoning and most of the stock.

3 Blend the cornflour with a little water, stir in the remaining stock and add to the pan.

4 Bring to the boil, stirring until thickened. Transfer the mixture to a warmed pie dish.

5 Mash the potatoes with half the butter and season well. Cover the meat with the potatoes and mark furrows with a fork.

6 Dot small pieces of the remaining butter over the top and bake in an oven preheated to 200°C/400°F/Gas Mark 6, for about 15 minutes or until the top is brown.

Cook's Notes

Time
Preparation takes 20 minutes and cooking takes about 20 minutes.

Preparation
Use raw mince and cook the mixture, covered, in the frying pan for about 20 minutes. Transfer to a heated pie dish. Top with hot mashed potato, dot with butter and brown under a preheated grill.

Variation
Add a little ground cinnamon to the meat for extra flavour.

PORK AND PEASE PUDDING

The peas absorb the flavour of the pork in this very old farmhouse dish – its origins can be traced back to the Middle Ages. Pickled pork was traditionally used but plain pork can be substituted.

SERVES 8

INGREDIENTS

1.8kg/4lb pickled hand and spring of pork
1 onion, sliced
2 carrots, peeled and sliced
2 small turnips, peeled and sliced
4 sticks celery, sliced
225g/8oz yellow split peas, soaked overnight
Sprig of sage
Sprig of thyme
Sprig of parsley
30g/1oz butter
1 egg yolk
Salt and pepper

1 Place the pork in a large saucepan with the onion, carrots, turnips and celery.
2 Place the soaked peas in a large piece of muslin. Tie into a bundle, leaving plenty of room for the peas to swell and expand. Add to the pan and tie to the handle with string.
3 Add the herbs and enough water to cover. Bring to the boil, then skim off any scum.
4 Reduce the heat and simmer, covered, for about 2 hours, or until the pork is tender.
5 When the pork is cooked, remove from the pan and keep warm. Remove the bag containing the peas and drain it well.
6 Purée the peas in a food processor or push through a sieve. Place the puréed peas in a clean pan over a gentle heat and beat in the butter and then the egg yolk. Season with salt and pepper and reheat gently.
7 To serve, strain some of the broth and serve as a gravy. Slice the pork and arrange on a serving dish. The vegetables can be served with the meat or as a soup with the remaining stock. Serve the pease pudding separately.

Cook's Notes

Time
Preparation takes about 30 minutes plus overnight soaking for the peas. Cooking takes about 2½ hours.

Buying Guide
Pickled pork is available from good butchers, but make sure you order it in advance.

CHOP TOAD-IN-THE-HOLE

Sausages in Yorkshire pudding batter, what everyone thinks of as toad-in-the-hole, is the modern-day version of this dish. The 'toad' originally consisted of lamb chops and kidneys.

<u>SERVES 6</u>

INGREDIENTS

BATTER
175g/6oz plain flour
Pinch of salt
2 large eggs
570ml/1 pint milk

2-3 tbsps fat (lard, dripping or oil)
6 small lamb chops
6 large pork sausages (more if wished)
½ medium onion, chopped

1 To make the batter, sift the flour and salt into a large mixing bowl and make a well in the centre. Break the eggs into the well and stir, slowly adding the milk and gradually incorporating the flour.

2 Beat well to form a smooth batter and leave the mixture to stand while your prepare the meat.
3 Melt 1-2 tbsps of the fat in a frying pan. Add the chops and sausages and cook for about 20 minutes until lightly browned, adding the onion about half way through.
4 Put the remaining 1 tbsp of fat in a baking tin and put in an oven preheated to 220°C/425°F/Gas Mark 7, for 3-5 minutes, or until very hot.
5 Remove from the oven, add the chops, sausages and onion and pour the batter around.
6 Return the tin to the oven and cook for 25-30 minutes or until the batter is set and the crust is well risen, brown and crisp.

Cook's Notes

Time
Preparation takes 30 minutes and cooking takes 25-30 minutes.

Serving Idea
Serve with gravy and a selection of vegetables.

Cook's Tip
The batter improves on standing.

ROAST LOIN OF PORK WITH SAGE AND ONION STUFFING BALLS

For many centuries pork was the mainstay of country folk, it was cheap to keep and, as the old saying goes, 'every part of the pig was used except for the squeak'.

<u>SERVES 6</u>

INGREDIENTS

1.4kg/3lb loin pork, boned and scored
Salt

SAGE AND ONION STUFFING BALLS
45g/1½oz butter
225g/8oz onions, finely chopped
A little stock or water
8 fresh sage leaves, finely chopped or 1 tsp dried sage
120g/4oz fresh white breadcrumbs
Salt and pepper
1 egg, beaten

1 Place the loin in a roasting tin. To ensure crisp crackling, rub salt well into the skin.

2 Cook in an oven preheated to 190°C/375°F/Gas Mark 5 for 1¾-2 hours, turning up the temperature to 200°C/400°F/Gas Mark 6 for the last 15 minutes, to finish off the crackling.

3 While the meat is cooking, melt the butter in a small saucepan and gently sauté the finely chopped onions for 3-4 minutes.

4 Add enough stock or water to just cover the onions, and simmer for 15 minutes.

5 Remove from the heat and add the sage, breadcrumbs and seasoning. Allow to cool slightly before adding the beaten egg.

6 Form the mixture into small balls and place them around the meat for the last 30 minutes of cooking.

Cook's Notes

Time
Preparation takes 30 minutes and cooking takes 1¾-2 hours.

Variation
The stuffing balls may be cooked separately, in a little oil on top of the stove.

Preparation
To ensure the skin of the pork crackles, it should be well scored at close intervals, down to the fat. The skin should be patted dry and salt rubbed into the scoring.

BRAISED OXTAIL

*Oxen were at one time used by farmers to pull
ploughs and carts, as they were stronger than horses.
The meat needs long slow cooking but will
produce a rich flavoured dish.*

SERVES 4

INGREDIENTS

900g-1.1kg/2-2½lbs of oxtail, jointed
Seasoned flour
30g/1oz dripping
2 carrots, peeled and sliced
2 large onions, finely sliced
1 rasher bacon, diced
Salt and pepper
2 bay leaves
2 parsley stalks
4 cloves
420ml/¾ pint game stock
140ml/¼ pint red wine

1 Dust the oxtail pieces with seasoned flour. Heat the dripping in a frying pan, add the oxtail, in batches, and fry until brown all over.
2 Remove from the pan and add the vegetables and bacon. Cook for 3-4 minutes, then place half the vegetables in a large casserole.
3 Set the meat on top and cover with the remaining vegetables. Season well and add the herbs and spices.
4 Pour in the stock and wine, bring nearly to the boil then cover and cook slowly in an oven preheated to 160°C/325°F/Gas Mark 3, for 2½-3 hours, or until the meat is tender.

Cook's Notes

Time
Preparation takes 30 minutes and cooking takes 2½-3 hours.

Preparation
If the gravy seems too thin, thicken it with some cornflour blended with a little water.

Serving Idea
Accompany with broccoli or cabbage and creamed potatoes.

STEAK AND KIDNEY PUDDING

Traditionally this pudding was brought to the table in the basin with a clean cloth or napkin wrapped around it.

SERVES 4-6

PASTRY

340g/12oz plain flour
Pinch of salt
2 tsps baking powder
175g/6oz shredded suet
About 200ml/7 fl oz water

FILLING

680g/1½lbs stewing steak
225g/8oz kidney
2 tbsps seasoned flour
175g/6oz mushrooms, quartered if large
280ml/½ pint beef stock

1 Sift the flour, salt and baking powder into a mixing bowl and stir in the suet. Add enough of the water to form a soft but not sticky dough.
2 Roll out the dough to form a circle, cut away a quarter of the pastry and reserve to make the lid of the pudding. Use the remaining three-quarters to line a 1.4-2.3 litre/3-4 pint greased pudding basin.
3 Cut the steak into cubes, discarding any fat or gristle. Remove the cores from the kidneys and cut into bite-size pieces. Toss the steak and kidney in the seasoned flour.
4 Place half the steak and kidney in the lined basin, then arrange a layer of mushrooms over the meat. Top with the remaining meat.
5 Pour the stock into the basin so that it comes to within about 2.5cm/1-inch of the top of the pastry. Any remaining stock can be heated up and served separately.
6 Dampen the edge of the pastry with water and roll out the reserved suet pastry to make a lid. Press the edges together well.
7 Cover the pudding with a sheet of buttered greaseproof paper and then foil, allowing enough room for the pudding to expand slightly. Tie the covering down with string.
8 Stand the basin in a large saucepan and add enough boiling water to come half way up the sides of the basin. Steam the pudding for 3-4 hours, boiling all the time and topping up the water level with more boiling water as necessary.

Cook's Notes

Time
Preparation takes 30 minutes and cooking takes 3-4 hours.

Serving Idea
Serve with a green vegetable and mashed or boiled potatoes, if wished.

LANCASHIRE HOT POT

Traditionally made in a lidded earthenware pot, this old farmhouse recipe was cooked when the oven was cooling down at the end of a baking day. In days when oysters were cheap and abundant a dozen were added to the dish.

SERVES 4-6

INGREDIENTS

900g/2lbs best end and middle neck of lamb, divided into cutlets
2 onions, sliced
900g/2lbs potatoes, thickly sliced
570ml/1 pint stock
1 bay leaf
½ tsp dried thyme
Salt and black pepper
Butter

1 In a large casserole, put layers of meat, onions and potatoes, ending with a thick layer of overlapping potatoes. Season the potatoes as you arrange them.

2 Pour over the stock and dot flecks of butter over the top layer of potatoes.
3 Cover with a tight-fitting lid and cook in an oven preheated to 180°C/350°F/Gas Mark 4, for 2-2½ hours.
4 Remove the casserole from the oven and turn the heat up to 200°C/400°F/Gas Mark 6. Take the lid off the casserole and dot the potatoes with more butter.
5 Return to the oven for 20-30 minutes uncovered, until the potatoes are crisp and lightly browned.

Cook's Notes

Time
Preparation takes 50 minutes and cooking takes 2½-3 hours.

Variation
If wished a little cornflour can be added to the stock for a thicker gravy.

KIDNEYS WITH BACON

Kidneys were once thought of as very humble, but by Victorian times their status had been elevated to the breakfast tables of the wealthy in the form of devilled kidneys.

SERVES 4

INGREDIENTS

460g/1lb lambs' kidneys
3 tbsps sherry
2 tbsps vegetable oil
8 rashers lean bacon, cut into 2.5cm/1-inch strips
1 onion, chopped
1 tbsp tomato chutney
1 tbsp Worcestershire sauce
2 tbsps water
Salt and freshly ground black pepper
1 tbsp cornflour
1½ tbsps fresh chopped parsley

1 Trim the fat from the kidneys and cut each kidney in half with a sharp knife.
2 Carefully trim out the hard core from the centre of each kidney using a sharp knife or scissors.
3 Cut a lattice design on the back of each kidney using a sharp knife, taking care not to cut right through them.

4 Put the kidneys into a bowl and stir in the sherry. Set aside for 15 minutes to marinate.
5 Heat the oil in a large frying pan and fry the bacon and onion for 5 minutes, stirring often to prevent burning. Remove from the pan and set aside.
6 Drain the kidneys and reserve the sherry marinade. Add the kidneys to the pan and cook for 3 minutes, stirring often.
7 Stir the tomato chutney, Worcestershire sauce and water into the pan with the kidneys, then add the bacon and onion mixture. Season with salt and pepper and fry gently for 5 minutes.
8 Blend the cornflour with the sherry marinade.
9 Add 1 tbsp parsley to the cornflour mixture and stir this into the kidneys in the pan, mixing well until the sauce is thickened and smooth. Serve at once, sprinkled with a little extra parsley.

Cook's Notes

Time
Preparation takes 20 minutes, cooking takes 15 minutes.

Watchpoint
Do not overcook the kidneys as they will become tough.

Cook's Tip
Cutting a lattice pattern into the kidneys helps them to cook quickly and evenly.

Serving Idea
Serve with creamed potatoes.

Beef Stew and Dumplings

Dumplings originated in Norfolk, where they were known as 'swimmers' or 'floaters'. Traditionally made with bread dough and not suet they were a staple food which soon became a nationwide favourite.

Serves 4-6

INGREDIENTS

460-675g/1-1½lbs stewing steak
30g/1oz dripping
2 onions, chopped
4 carrots, sliced
1 bay leaf
30g/1oz seasoned flour
850ml/1½ pints brown stock
Pinch of mixed herbs
Salt and pepper

DUMPLINGS

175g/6oz self-raising flour
½ tsp salt
90g/3oz shredded suet
Water to mix

1 Cut the meat into cubes, removing any excess fat.
2 Heat half the fat in an oven- and flameproof casserole and add the onions, carrots and bay leaf.
3 Cook for 3-5 minutes to soften, then remove from the dish with a slotted spoon. Add the remaining fat to the casserole and reheat.

4 Coat the meat in seasoned flour and fry in the fat in batches for a few minutes to seal.
5 Add the vegetables and stir in the stock, herbs and seasoning. Bring to boiling point. Cover and transfer to an oven preheated to 180°C/350°F/Gas Mark 4. Cook for 2½ hours or until the meat is tender.
6 Meanwhile, make the dumplings. Sieve the flour and salt into a basin.
7 Add the suet and blend with a knife. Stir in enough water to bind. The dumpling mixture should be just soft enough to form into balls.
8 Divide into 8 portions and roll into balls with lightly floured hands.
9 Add to the stew 20 minutes before the end of the cooking time, putting them into the simmering liquid.
10 Serve as soon as the dumplings are cooked.

Cook's Notes

Time
Preparation takes about 30 minutes and cooking takes 2½ hours.

Preparation
If necessary, the gravy can be thickened with a little cornflour mixed with water, before the dumplings are added.

Cook's Tip
Make sure the casserole is large enough to accommodate the dumplings as well as the stew.

Variation
Add some kidney to the stew if you like, this will help to thicken the gravy.

BEEF OLIVES

*Beef olives (slices of beef wrapped around a herb stuffing)
first appeared in English cookery in the middle ages.*

SERVES 4

INGREDIENTS

8 thin beef frying steaks, about 10 x 15cm/4 x 6 inches
30g/1oz shredded suet
2 rashers streaky bacon, rind removed, chopped
120g/4oz fresh white breadcrumbs
2 tsps chopped fresh parsley
½ tsp dried mixed herbs
Grated rind of ½ lemon
Salt and pepper
1 small egg, beaten
Seasoned flour
30g/1oz butter
420ml/¾ pint beef stock
2 tbsps sherry

1 Place the steaks between two sheets of dampened greaseproof paper and pound them with a meat mallet or rolling pin to flatten slightly.

2 Place the suet, bacon, breadcrumbs, parsley, mixed herbs, lemon rind, seasoning and egg in a mixing bowl and beat until well combined.

3 Divide the stuffing into 8 and place a portion on each piece of beef. Roll up and secure with string, then dust with seasoned flour.

4 Melt the butter in a frying pan and fry the olives until browned on all sides. Remove from the pan and place in a shallow ovenproof dish.

5 Stir 2 tbsps seasoned flour into the pan and cook over a low heat, stirring constantly until brown. Gradually stir in the stock and cook until thickened slightly.

6 Stir in the sherry, then pour over the beef olives. Cover and cook in an oven preheated to 180°C/350°F/ Gas Mark 4, for 45-50 minutes.

7 Carefully remove the meat to a serving dish and cut off the string. Pour the sauce over the beef olives and serve immediately.

8 The sauce should be of a coating consistency, if it is too thin, transfer to a pan and boil until reduced slightly, if too thick, stir in a little extra beef stock.

Cook's Notes

Time
Preparation takes 35-45 minutes and cooking takes about 1 hour.

Variation
Large veal escalopes may be used instead of beef.

CHAPTER FIVE

PUDDINGS
&
DESSERTS

BAKED APPLE DUMPLINGS

*Stuffed baked apples are an old country dish.
Surrounded in pastry sweetened with cinnamon and spices
this makes a deliciously warming winter dessert.*

<u>SERVES 6</u>

INGREDIENTS

340g/12oz plain flour
¼ tsp salt
¼ tsp cinnamon
¼ tsp ground nutmeg
175g/6oz butter, diced
75-105ml/5-7 tbsps iced water
6 medium-sized dessert apples
6 prunes, pitted
6 dried apricots
2 tbsps raisins
1 egg, beaten to glaze
Sugar

1 Sift the flour, salt and spices into a large bowl. Rub the butter into the flour until the mixture resembles fine breadcrumbs.
2 Mix in enough of the water to produce a smooth pliable dough. Divide the dough into six pieces and roll out into 20cm/8-inch squares.

3 Peel the apples and carefully remove the centre cores with an apple corer.
4 Chop the prunes and the apricots and mix these with the raisins.
5 Place one prepared apple into the centre of each pastry square and fill the cavities with equal amounts of the dried fruit mixture.
6 Brush the edges of each square with a little water, and draw them up and around the sides of the apples, sealing them well and trimming off any excess pastry to give a neat finish.
7 Roll out the pastry trimmings, cut into decorative leaves and stick the leaves onto each apple for decoration.
8 Glaze each pastry apple with the beaten egg and sprinkle with a little sugar. Place on a lightly greased baking sheet.
9 Bake the apples in an oven preheated to 160°C/350°F/Gas Mark 4, for 20-25 minutes or until golden brown.

Cook's Notes

Time
Preparation takes approximately 30 minutes, cooking takes 20-25 minutes.

Cook's Tip
For an extra rich pastry, use 1 egg yolk and half the amount of water in this recipe.

Variation
Use cooking apples and add 2 tbsps sugar with the dried fruit. Alternatively stuff with mincemeat.

Serving Idea
Serve with cream or home-made custard.

BAKEWELL TART

This popular dish was created by complete accident in Bakewell, a small village in Derbyshire. The cook of a local inn made the mistake of spreading the butter, sugar and egg mixture over the top of a jam tart, when it was supposed to have been added to the pastry to make a rich crust. In Derbyshire, the dish is still called by its original name of Bakewell Pudding.

SERVES 8

INGREDIENTS

175g/6oz shortcrust pastry
2-3 tbsps raspberry jam
120g/4oz butter
120g/4oz caster sugar
½ tsp vanilla essence
A few drops of almond essence
Grated rind and juice of ½ lemon
2 large eggs
90g/3oz crumbs (from trifle sponges, Madeira cake or fresh
   white bread)
90g/3oz ground almonds
½ tsp baking powder
1 tbsp milk

1 Roll the pastry out thinly and use to line a 900ml/1½ pint greased, shallow pie dish. Save any trimmings for decoration.

2 Spread the jam over the pastry.

3 Cream the butter and sugar together in a mixing bowl until light and fluffy. Add the flavourings and lemon rind and juice, then beat in the eggs until well blended.

4 Mix the cake crumbs and ground almonds together and fold into the mixture. Add the baking powder and milk.

5 Pour this mixture over the jam and decorate the top with pastry strips made from the trimmings.

6 Bake in an oven preheated to 200°C/400°F/Gas Mark 6, for 15 minutes. Reduce the temperature to 180°C/350°F/Gas Mark 4 and bake for a further 20-25 minutes, or until the tart is golden brown and firm to the touch.

Cook's Notes

Time
Preparation takes 15 minutes and cooking takes 35-40 minutes.

Preparation
Cook the tart in a greased 20.5cm/8-inch flan tin. Strawberry or plum jam will also work well in this dish.

Variation
Instead of decorating the tart with strips of pastry, coat with glacé icing (when cool) and decorate with toasted flaked almond.

QUEEN OF PUDDINGS

It is not known where or when the name of this pudding originated, but it certainly lives up to its title!

<u>SERVES 4-6</u>

INGREDIENTS

3 medium slices of white bread
420ml/¾ pint milk
30g/1oz butter
Grated rind of 1 lemon
120g/4oz caster sugar
3 eggs, separated
2 tbsps seedless raspberry jam, warmed

1 Cut off and discard the crusts of the bread. Tear the slices into pieces.
2 Heat the milk with the butter. When simmering, remove the pan from the heat and add the bread, lemon rind and 30g/1oz of the sugar.
3 Allow to stand for 10-15 minutes then beat the mixture until smooth. Beat in egg yolks, one at a time, until well blended.

4 Grease an 850ml-1.14 litre/1½-2 pint ovenproof glass dish and pour the mixture into it.
5 Bake in an oven preheated to 180°C/350°F/Gas Mark 4, for about 25 minutes, or until set.
6 Spread the jam gently over the top, being careful not to break the surface.
7 Whisk the egg whites until stiff, add half the remaining caster sugar and whisk again until glossy. Gently fold in the rest of the sugar using a metal spoon.
8 Spoon the meringue over the pudding, making sure to cover it right up to the edges and lifting the spoon to form small peaks.
9 Return the dish to the oven for about 10 minutes until the peaks are a golden brown. Serve hot or warm.

Cook's Notes

Time
Preparation takes 20 minutes cooking takes about 40 minutes.

Variation
Use strawberry or apricot jam instead of raspberry.

TRIFLE

*Trifle became popular in the 18th century
and consisted of cake or biscuits soaked
in wine and covered with syllabub.*

SERVES 8

INGREDIENTS

*1 packet trifle sponge cakes, split in half or ½ packet, plus
60g/2oz macaroons
Raspberry jam
Dry sherry
225-340g/8-12oz fresh raspberries
280ml/½ pint double cream
Toasted flaked almonds*

CUSTARD

*4 tbsps cornflour
60g/2oz vanilla sugar
570ml/1 pint milk
2 eggs, lightly beaten
2 tbsps dry sherry*

1 Sandwich together the sponges with plenty of raspberry jam. Arrange in the bottom of a large glass dish.

2 Spoon over plenty of sherry to soak the sponge. Place the fruit layer over the sponge.

3 To make the custard, place the cornflour and sugar in a mixing bowl and blend in 60ml/4 tbsps of the milk.

4 Bring the rest of the milk nearly to the boil and pour onto the cornflour mixture, stirring constantly. Return the mixture to the pan and bring to the boil, stirring.

5 Simmer for 1 minute, remove from the heat and beat in the eggs and sherry. Leave to cool until lukewarm, then pour over the raspberries. Chill.

6 Whip the cream until soft peaks form then spread over the custard. Decorate the top with toasted flaked almonds and serve.

Cook's Notes

Time
Preparation takes 20 minutes, plus chilling time and cooking takes 5 minutes.

Variation
Add other fresh fruits such as bananas, peaches or strawberries.

RHUBARB FOOL

*Rhubarb is the first fresh 'fruit' (it is actually
a vegetable) of the year and this dish makes
a delicious and indulgent dessert.*

SERVES 6

INGREDIENTS

460g/1lb rhubarb
60g/2oz sugar
2-3 strips of lemon rind
280ml/½ pint whipping cream
Lemon rind and mint to decorate

1 Trim and scrub the rhubarb and cut into 2.5cm/1-inch lengths. Place in a buttered ovenproof dish.

2 Add the sugar, lemon rind and about 3 tbsps water. Cover and cook in an oven preheated to 150°C/300°F/Gas Mark 2 for about 40 minutes or until the rhubarb is soft.

3 Purée in a blender and allow to cool. Whip the cream until soft peaks form then fold into the rhubarb purée.

4 Chill before serving. Decorate with strips of lemon rind and mint leaves.

Cook's Notes

Time
Preparation takes 15 minutes and cooking takes 40 minutes.

Variation
The fool can be made with half custard and half cream.

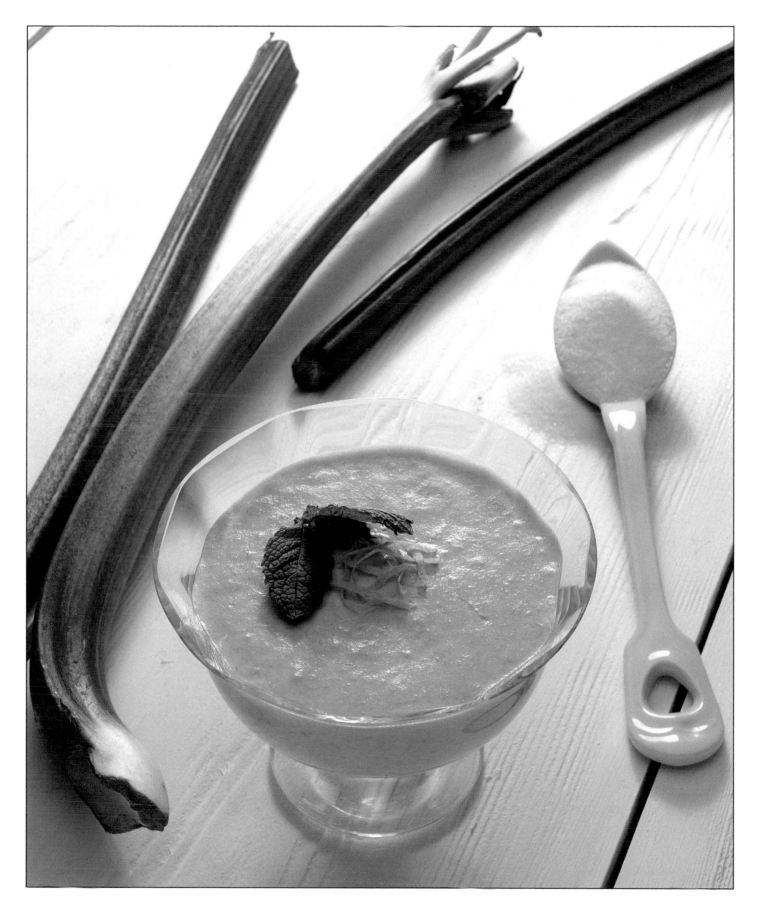

GOOSEBERRY PIE

In a small area in Gloucestershire, gooseberry pies made with a hot-water pastry were traditionally eaten at Whitsuntide.

<u>SERVES 8</u>

INGREDIENTS

PASTRY
275g/10oz plain flour
Pinch of salt
75g/2½oz butter, cut into small pieces
75g/2½oz lard, cut into small pieces
2½ tbsps cold water

FILLING
900g/2lbs gooseberries, topped and tailed
225g/8oz granulated sugar
Milk or beaten egg to glaze
Single cream or custard, to serve

1 Sift the flour with the salt into a mixing bowl. Add the butter and lard, and rub in until the mixture resembles breadcrumbs.
2 Stir in the water and form into a firm dough.

3 Roll out half the pastry on a lightly floured surface and use it to line a 20cm/8-inch pie dish.
4 Place the gooseberries in a saucepan with a little water and simmer for 5-6 minutes. Remove from the heat and leave to cool.
5 Strain the fruit well, then mix with the sugar. Spoon into the prepared pastry case.
6 Roll out the remaining pastry and cover the pie. Dampen the edges and seal together. Any excess pastry can be used to make leaves to decorate.
7 Make a small hole in the centre of the pie and brush the pastry with milk or beaten egg.
8 Place on baking tray and cook in an oven preheated to 200°C/400°F/Gas Mark 6, for 20 minutes then reduce the oven temperature to 190°C/375°F/Gas Mark 5, and cook for a further 15-20 minutes or until the gooseberries are tender.

Cook's Notes

Time
Preparation takes 20 minutes and cooking takes about 45 minutes.

Preparation
If the pie crust starts to get too brown cover it with a double thickness of greaseproof paper.

Variation
A sprig of elderflower can be added to the gooseberries when cooking in the saucepan. Remove the sprig before cooling the berries.

TREACLE TART

*This old-fashioned favourite was
originally made with treacle, but golden syrup
is the more usual ingredient today.*

SERVES 4-6

INGREDIENTS

225g/8oz shortcrust pastry
175g/6oz golden syrup
2 tbsps lemon juice
60g/2oz fresh white breadcrumbs

1 Roll out the pastry and use to line a 20cm/8-inch shallow pie plate. Reserve any trimmings.
2 In a small pan, warm the syrup and lemon juice over a low heat, stir in the breadcrumbs and pour over the pastry case.

3 Roll out the pastry trimmings and cut into thin strips. Use these to make a lattice pattern over the syrup filling.
4 Dampen the ends of the strips and press them lightly onto the edge of the tart.
5 Bake in the centre of an oven preheated to 190°C/375°F/Gas Mark 5, for 25-30 minutes, until the pastry is cooked and the filling golden and firm.

Cook's Notes

Time
Preparation takes 15 minutes and cooking takes 25-30 minutes.

Variation
Add ¼ tsp ground ginger to the filling for extra flavour.

Serving Idea
Serve hot or cold with cream or custard.

YORKSHIRE APPLE PIE

'Apple pie without cheese is like a kiss without a squeeze'.
This is an old saying from North Yorkshire where traditional
Wensleydale cheese has been made since the twelfth century.
The cheese can be served separately to accompany
the pie or, like this recipe, baked in it.

SERVES 4-6

INGREDIENTS

275g/10oz shortcrust pastry
340g/12oz cooking apples, peeled, cored and sliced
2 tbsps sugar
120g/4oz strong cheese, roughly crumbled
1 tbsp water
Little milk and sugar to glaze

1 Roll out the pastry and use two-thirds to line a 20cm/8-inch flan ring.

2 Toss the apples with the sugar and cheese. Use to fill the pastry case. Sprinkle the apples with the water.
3 Roll out the remaining pastry to make a lid. Cover the apples and seal the edges.
4 Make a couple of slits in the centre of the pastry to let the steam out. Brush the top with a little milk and sprinkle with sugar.
5 Place in an oven preheated to 190°C/375°F/ Gas Mark 5, and bake for 35-40 minutes, or until the crust is firm and lightly browned.

Cook's Notes

Time
Preparation takes 20 minutes and cooking takes about 40 minutes.

Serving Idea
Serve hot or warm with whipped cream.

SPOTTED DICK

This traditional childhood favourite, although not as frequently served these days, is a wonderful way of indulging in a nice sticky pudding.

SERVES 6-8

INGREDIENTS

225g/8oz plain flour
1½ tsps baking powder
¼ tsp ground mixed spice
Pinch of salt
120g/4oz shredded suet
120g/4oz soft brown sugar
120g/4oz currants
140ml/¼ pint milk
Flour for dusting

1 Sift the flour, baking powder, mixed spice and salt into a mixing bowl. Stir in the suet, sugar and currants until well combined.
2 Add enough milk to form a soft but not sticky dough. Lightly flour a work surface and shape the mixture into a roll.

3 Liberally sprinkle a piece of greaseproof paper with flour and place the dough on the paper. Roll up and twist the ends to seal. Wrap the roll in a clean tea-towel or pudding cloth and secure the ends with string.
4 Place the roll in a large saucepan and add enough water to come about half way up the side of the pudding. Bring to the boil, then reduce the heat. Cover and simmer for 1½ hours, topping up the water level with more boiling water as necessary.
5 When cooked, remove the pudding from the pan and unwrap. Slice, and serve with plenty of creamy custard.

Cook's Notes

Time
Preparation takes about 30 minutes and cooking takes 1½ hours.

Variation
Shape the pudding into a round a cook for an extra ¾-1 hour.

CREAMY RICE PUDDING

*Nothing can beat a traditional creamy rice pudding
for dessert on a cold winter day.*

<u>SERVES 4</u>

INGREDIENTS

200g/7oz short- or medium-grain rice
Nutmeg
120g/4oz sugar
Pinch of salt
1 litre/1¾ pints scalded milk

---

1 Wash and drain the rice well. Put it into a greased baking dish and grate over a little nutmeg to taste.

2 Sprinkle over the sugar and the salt, then pour in the scalded milk. Do not stir.
3 Bake the pudding in an oven preheated to 180°C/350°F/Gas Mark 4, for about 1½ hours. Do not stir. When ready, the rice grains should show above the milk and the milk should be thick and creamy.

Cook's Notes

Time
Preparation takes 10 minutes and cooking takes 1½ hours.

Serving Idea
Serve with stewed fruit, jam or golden syrup.

SUMMER PUDDING

*This classic British dessert was devised as an
ingenious and delicious way of using up stale bread.*

SERVES 6-8

INGREDIENTS

*680g/1½lbs mixed, fresh soft fruit, eg. raspberries, redcurrants
and strawberries*
120g/4oz granulated sugar
9-10 slices white bread, thickly cut and with crusts removed

1 Put all the fruit into a saucepan with the sugar and heat gently until the sugar has dissolved and the juices run, but the fruit is not completely cooked. Shake the pan whilst heating instead of stirring, to ensure the fruit stays as whole as possible.

2 Remove the pan from the heat and leave the fruit to cool.

3 Line the base and sides of a 900ml/1½-pint pudding basin with 6 or 7 slices of the bread, trying not to leave any gaps between each slice. Cut the slices to fit, as necessary.

4 Spoon the fruit mixture into the centre of the pudding adding a little of the juice. Cover the top completely with the remaining bread slices. Reserve the remaining juice.

5 Press the top bread slices down firmly and place a saucer, or small plate, on top of the pudding. Weight the plate down with a heavy weight.

6 Chill the pudding in the refrigerator overnight. Turn the pudding out of the bowl carefully, and spoon over the remaining juice to stain the bread.

Cook's Notes

Time
Preparation takes about 10-15 minutes, plus overnight chilling time.

Cook's Tip
If you do not have a heavy weight handy, a bag of sugar, or flour, will do equally well.

EVERLASTING SYLLABUB

*This syllabub got its name from its ability to stand
in the glass for several days without deflating.
Originally the term syllabub was applied to the mixture made
by adding milk – directly from the cow – to a mug
of ale or wine, to produce a foamy drink.*

SERVES 4

INGREDIENTS

140ml/¼ pint white wine
2 tbsps brandy
Grated rind and juice of 1 lemon
60g/2oz caster sugar
280ml/½ pint double cream
Grated nutmeg

1 Stir the wine, brandy, lemon rind and juice together
and allow to stand for at least 2 hours.

2 Stir in the caster sugar and stir until dissolved.
3 Place the double cream in a mixing bowl and whisk
with a balloon whisk until beginning to thicken.
4 Gradually whisk in the wine mixture. When all the
wine has been added, continue to whisk until the
mixture stands in soft peaks.
5 Spoon into glasses and grate a little nutmeg on top.
Chill before serving.

Cook's Notes

Time
Preparation takes
about 25 minutes plus 2
hours standing time. Chill
before serving.

Variation
Substitute a small
orange for the lemon and
rum or sherry for the
brandy.

Serving Idea
Use as a topping for
Trifle.

Sweet Almond Pudding

*A delicious variation on a traditional pudding;
ground rice was never like this at school!*

Serves 4

INGREDIENTS
175g/6oz blanched almonds
420ml/¾ pint water
175g/6oz sugar
3 tbsps ground rice
140ml/¼ pint milk

1 Blend the blanched almonds and the water in a liquidiser or food processor until the almonds are well chopped.

2 Put the almond liquid into a medium-sized saucepan and bring this mixture to the boil over a gentle heat. Add the sugar and stir until it has completely dissolved.
3 Blend together the rice and milk in a jug. Add the rice mixture slowly to the simmering sugar and almond mixture, stirring continuously until the pudding thickens.
4 Remove the rice pudding from the heat and pour into individual serving dishes.

Cook's Notes

Time
Preparation takes about 5 minutes and cooking takes 6-7 minutes.

Variation
Lightly toast some flaked or chopped almonds and sprinkle over the top of the pudding to serve.

Serving Idea
Serve this pudding hot or cold with fresh or stewed fruit or jam.

DE-LUXE BREAD AND BUTTER PUDDING

This favourite winter pudding is an excellent way of using up stale bread. Serve just as it is, hot from the oven.

SERVES 4

INGREDIENTS

4 thin slices, white or wholemeal bread
A little butter
Raspberry jam, optional
2 eggs
420ml/¾ pint milk, warmed
2 tbsps single cream
3 tbsps light muscovado sugar
1 tsp vanilla essence
2 tbsps sultanas, soaked for 1 hour
1 tbsp chopped dates
Grated nutmeg

1 Remove the crusts from the bread.
2 Sandwich the bread with the butter and jam, if using, and cut into small triangles.

3 Beat the eggs until fluffy.
4 Add the warmed milk, cream, sugar and vanilla.
5 Stir together well, making sure that the sugar has dissolved.
6 Arrange the bread triangles in a lightly buttered ovenproof dish so that they overlap and stand up slightly.
7 Scatter the dried fruits over the top.
8 Pour the egg, cream and milk mixture into the dish, ensuring that the bread triangles are saturated.
9 Grate a little nutmeg over the pudding and bake in an oven preheated to 200°C/400°F/Gas Mark 6 for about 30 minutes.

Cook's Notes

Time
Preparation takes 10 minutes and cooking takes 30 minutes.

Variation
Use other flavoured jams such as apricot instead of raspberry.

Preparation
If using stale bread, allow the pudding to stand for 20-30 minutes before baking to allow it to soak up the liquid.

STEAMED RASPBERRY JAM PUDDING

Originally puddings like this were boiled in a pudding cloth, not steamed in a basin. The invention of the pudding cloth in the 1600s was quite an event in culinary terms, sparking off a whole variety of new pudding recipes.

SERVES 6

INGREDIENTS

120g/4oz raspberry jam
120g/4oz butter
120g/4oz sugar
2 eggs
1 tsp vanilla essence
120g/4oz plain flour
1 tsp baking powder
2 tbsps milk

1 Grease a heatproof 900ml/1½-pint pudding basin thoroughly with butter. Put the jam into the bottom of the mould and set aside.
2 Cream the measured butter with the sugar until light and fluffy.
3 Beat in the eggs one at a time and add the vanilla essence. Sift in the flour and baking powder and then fold in using a metal tablespoon. If the mixture is too stiff, add up to 2 tbsps of milk to make a soft dropping consistency. Spoon the sponge mixture carefully on to the jam in the basin and smooth the surface.
4 Cut a large square of greaseproof paper and foil for covering the basin. Grease one side of the paper and place the foil on top, on the non-greased side. Fold a 2.5cm/1-inch pleat down the centre of the double layer of covering and place on top of the basin. Tie it in place under the rim of the basin with some string.
5 Place the pudding in the top of a double steamer over boiling water and cover. Steam for 2 hours checking the level of the water regularly and topping it up with more boiling water when necessary. (If you do not have a double steamer, stand the pudding in a large saucepan and pour enough boiling water around the pudding to come half way up the sides of the basin. Cover and steam as above.)
6 Remove the pudding from the steamer and take off the covering. Slide a round-bladed knife round the edge to loosen the pudding. Hold a warmed serving plate on top of the basin then invert and remove the basin.

Cook's Notes

Time
Preparation takes 15-20 minutes and cooking takes 2 hours.

Serving Idea
Serve with custard and extra warmed jam.

Variation
Make a treacle pudding by substituting golden syrup for the jam.

CHAPTER SIX

BAKING

BARA BRITH

*This sweet bread is a traditional farmhouse recipe from North Wales.
The name means speckled bread and was originally a rich
sweet version of an every day loaf, baked for special occasions
such as Easter and Christmas.*

<u>MAKES 2 LOAVES</u>

INGREDIENTS

½ tsp salt
½ tsp cinnamon
Pinch of grated nutmeg
460g/1lb strong white flour
60g/2oz sugar
1 tbsp fast-acting yeast
60g/2oz butter
1 egg, lightly beaten
225ml/8 fl oz milk, at room temperature
175g/6oz sultanas
150g/5oz currants
90g/3oz chopped mixed peel

1 Add the salt and spices to the flour and sift into a large mixing bowl. Stir in the sugar and yeast and rub in the butter.

2 Add the egg to the milk. Make a well in the centre of the flour and pour in the liquid. Gradually incorporate the flour into the liquid, beating it in well until the dough becomes stiff and elastic.

3 Put the dough in a large greased bowl and cover with a damp, clean cloth. Leave in a warm place for 1–2 hours to allow the dough to rise.

4 When the mixture has doubled in volume lightly knead in the dried fruit and peel.

5 Divide the mixture between two greased loaf tins about 21.5cm x 11cm/8½- x 4½-inches, or two 18cm/7-inch cake tins.

6 Cover again and allow to rise for 30 minutes.

7 Bake in the centre of an oven preheated to 190°C/375°F/Gas Mark 5, for 35-45 minutes or until a skewer inserted into the centre of the loaves comes out clean. Turn out of the tins and cool on a wire rack.

Cook's Notes

Time
Preparation takes 20 minutes plus 1½-2½ hours rising time. Cooking takes 35-45 minutes.

Preparation
The loaves may be glazed with 1 tbsp sugar dissolved in 4 tbsps hot water when cooked and put back in the oven for 5 minutes with the heat turned down.

Variation
The loaves may be shaped by hand into rounds or oblongs and cooked on a baking sheet instead of in tins.

FRUIT SCONES

A country-wide favourite for afternoon tea,
scones are at their best when served with home-made
jam and that West Country delight, clotted cream.

SERVES 10-12

INGREDIENTS

225g/8oz plain flour
1 tsp cream of tartar
½ tsp bicarbonate of soda
¼ tsp salt
60g/2oz butter
90g/3oz sultanas
30g/1oz sugar
2 eggs, beaten
Milk for blending
Beaten egg, for glaze

1 Mix the flour, cream of tartar, bicarbonate of soda and salt together and sieve it twice through a metal sieve to aerate it completely.

2 Put the sieved flour into a large bowl and rub in the butter until the mixture resembles fine breadcrumbs.
3 Stir in the sultanas and sugar. Add the beaten eggs, mixing well to form a soft dough. Add a little milk if the dough is too stiff.
4 Lightly flour a work surface. Turn out the dough and knead it lightly until it becomes smooth.
5 Roll the dough out until it is about 1.25cm/ ½-inch thick and cut into 5cm/2-inch rounds using a biscuit cutter.
6 Place the scones on a greased baking sheet and brush each one with the extra beaten egg.
7 Bake in an oven preheated to 200°C/400°F/ Gas Mark 6, for 10-15 minutes, or until golden brown and well risen.

Cook's Notes

Time
Preparation takes about 15 minutes, cooking takes 10-15 minutes.

Preparation
Do not roll the dough out too thinly, otherwise the scones will not rise properly.

Variation
Make cheese scones by substituting grated cheese for the sugar and omitting the sultanas.

VICTORIA SANDWICH CAKE

*Named after Queen Victoria, this cake was first served
at her tea-parties before it became a national favourite.*

SERVES 6-8

INGREDIENTS

120g/4oz butter or margarine
120g/4oz caster sugar
2 large eggs
A few drops of vanilla essence
120g/4oz self-raising flour, sifted

TO FINISH
Raspberry jam and sifted icing sugar

1 In a medium-sized mixing bowl, cream together the butter and sugar until light and fluffy. Beat in the eggs one at a time and the vanilla essence.

2 Using a metal spoon, gently fold in the sifted flour. When it is all incorporated, divide the mixture equally between two greased and lined 18cm/7-inch straight sided sandwich tins, levelling off the surface.

3 Bake in the centre of an oven preheated to 180°C/350°F/Gas Mark 4, for about 25 minutes. Test by pressing a finger gently onto the sponge – it should feel springy and leave no impression.

4 Leave to cool for a minute in the tins, then turn out onto wire cooling racks. Carefully peel off the greaseproof paper.

5 When cold, sandwich the two layers together with jam and dust the top with sifted icing sugar.

Cook's Notes

Time
Preparation takes 20 minutes and cooking takes about 25 minutes.

Variation
Sandwich with other jams or lemon curd, adding grated rind to the cake mixture. Whipped cream may be added on top of the jam filling.

POUND CAKE

*This rich cake is made with equal weights of flour,
fat, sugar and eggs. Variations of this cake abound, but
the traditional recipe, using a flavouring of vanilla essence or
orange flower water, is the most outstanding.*

SERVES 8

INGREDIENTS

275g/10oz softened butter
275g/10oz sugar
½ tsp vanilla essence or 1 tbsp orange flower water
5 eggs
1 tbsp baking powder
275g/10oz plain flour

1 Beat the butter, sugar and vanilla (if using), together
in a mixing bowl until light and fluffy.

2 Beat in the eggs one at a time, together with the
orange flower water (if using) and the baking powder.
Gradually beat in the flour to obtain a thick batter.

3 Pour the cake batter into either a non-stick or a
greased a lined loaf tin and bake in an oven preheated
to 180°C/350°F/Gas Mark 4, for about 45 minutes or
until a skewer inserted into the centre comes out clean.

Cook's Notes

Time
Preparation takes 15
minutes and cooking takes
about 45 minutes.

Variation
Chopped hazelnuts
or walnuts may be added
to the cake batter.

Serving Idea
Decorate with glacé
icing.

GINGERBREAD

*There are many types of gingerbread still made throughout
the country, some with treacle, some with golden syrup and others
with a mixture of both. Recipes even include mixed peel, as in
Grasmere gingerbread from the Lake District, as well as
oatmeal which is a crucial ingredient in Yorkshire parkin.*

MAKES ONE 17.5CM/7-INCH SQUARE CAKE

INGREDIENTS
120g/4oz unsalted butter
120ml/4 fl oz black treacle
225g/8oz light soft brown sugar
120ml/4 fl oz hot water
300g/10oz plain flour
2 tsps baking powder
2 tsps ground ginger
A little grated nutmeg
1 egg, beaten

1 Put the butter into a large saucepan with the treacle and sugar. Heat gently, stirring all the time, until the sugar and butter have melted together.

2 Pour in the hot water, mix well and set aside.

3 Sift the flour with the baking powder and ginger into a large bowl. Make a well in the centre and add the nutmeg and beaten egg.

4 Gradually beat in the treacle mixture using a wooden spoon and drawing the flour from the outside into the centre gradually.

5 Pour the gingerbread mixture into a greased and lined 17.5cm/7-inch square cake tin and bake in an oven preheated to 160°C/325°F/Gas Mark 3, for about 1 hour, or until a skewer inserted into the cake comes out clean.

6 Allow the cake to cool in the tin, before turning out onto a wire rack and cutting into squares.

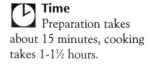

Cook's Notes

Time
Preparation takes about 15 minutes, cooking takes 1-1½ hours.

Variation
Add 60g/2oz chopped, mixed fruit to the gingerbread mixture along with the spices.

Serving Idea
Serve as a dessert with a lemon sauce or coat with glacé icing.

SCOTTISH SHORTBREAD

*In Scotland, shortbread is traditionally associated with Hogmanay.
'First-footers', the first people to enter a house after the stroke of midnight,
(traditionally carrying a lump of coal) are said to bring good luck to the
householder, and are offered shortbread as a token of thanks.*

MAKES 6-8 WEDGES

INGREDIENTS
120g/4oz butter
60g/2oz caster sugar
120g/4oz plain flour
60g/2oz rice flour

1 In a bowl, cream together the butter and sugar.
2 Add the sifted flours and, using your fingers, lightly mix in all the ingredients until they change from a crumbly texture to a dough.
3 Roll out or press the dough into a circle about 1.25cm/½-inch thick and place on a greased baking sheet. Alternatively, press into a shortbread mould or a baking tin.
4 Mark out the surface into wedges or fingers, depending on the mould or tin shape and prick all over with a fork.
5 Bake in an oven preheated to 180°C/350°F/Gas Mark 4, for 40-45 minutes or until pale golden.
6 Cool slightly then remove from the mould or tin and leave to cool completely on a wire rack.

Cook's Notes

Time
Preparation takes 15 minutes and cooking takes 40-45 minutes.

Cook's Tip
Store in an airtight container. If wished, the shortbread can be made with all plain flour. The addition of rice flour makes it more crisp in texture.

Buying Guide
Decorative shortbread moulds are available from specialist kitchen shops.

SCOFA BREAD

*The ideal chunky bread to serve warm with
a ploughman's lunch or lunchtime salad meals.*

MAKES 1 LOAF

INGREDIENTS

570ml/1¼lbs self-raising wholemeal flour
225g/8oz bran
1 tsp salt
120g/4oz butter or vegetable fat
Just under 570ml/1 pint water
1 tbsp vegetable oil

1 Put the flour, bran and salt into a mixing bowl.
2 Rub in the fat and mix the water and oil together.
3 Make a well in the centre of the flour and pour in the water and oil.

4 Mix in the flour, drawing it into the liquid mixture gradually from the sides until a dough is formed.
5 Shape into an 8cm/7-inch round and place on a greased baking tray.
6 With a sharp knife cut to within 1.25cm/½-inch of the bottom, making four sections.
7 Bake just above the centre of an oven preheated to 200°C/400°F/Gas Mark 6 for about 1 hour or until nicely browned and 'hollow' sounding when tapped underneath with the knuckles.
8 Remove from the oven and wrap in a clean tea-towel to cool.

Cook's Notes

Time
Preparation takes 10 minutes, cooking takes 1 hour.

Cook's Tip
Eat within a couple of days.

GRIDDLE SCONES

*Also known as drop scones or Scotch pancakes, these
cakes are delicious served straight from the griddle.
The Welsh traditionally serve raspberries with plain griddle scones.*

<u>SERVES 4-6</u>

INGREDIENTS

120g/4oz self-raising flour
Pinch of salt
45g/1½oz butter
120g/4oz currants
½ tsp ground nutmeg
1 egg
90ml/3 fl oz milk

1 Mix the flour and salt together, and rub in the butter until the mixture resembles fine breadcrumbs.
2 Stir in the currants and the nutmeg, then push the mixture gently to the sides of the bowl to form a well in the centre.

3 Beat together the egg and the milk and pour into the well in the centre of the flour.
4 Using a wooden spoon, mix the egg and milk mixture into the flour, stirring from the centre of the bowl and gradually drawing the flour in from the sides to form a smooth, thick batter.
5 Heat a griddle or heavy-based frying pan over a moderate heat and grease with a little butter.
6 Drop tablespoons of the batter into the hot pan, spacing them out well, and cook for 2-3 minutes, or until the bases are set and have turned golden brown.
7 Turn the scones over using a palette knife and cook on the other side in the same way.

Cook's Notes

Time
Preparation takes 15 minutes, cooking takes about 4 minutes per scone.

Preparation
If the batter is too thick, add a little extra milk until it becomes a soft dropping consistency.

Serving Idea
Serve with jam, butter and sugar or golden syrup.

RICH FRUIT CAKE

This cake was popular served for afternoon tea in Victorian days.
For a special occasion it can be covered with marzipan and icing.

<u>MAKES 1 X 20.5CM/8-INCH CAKE</u>

INGREDIENTS

650g/1lb 7oz mixed dried fruit
90g/3oz glace cherries, quartered
60g/2oz flaked almonds
175g/6oz butter
175g/6oz light muscovado sugar
3 eggs (size 2), beaten
215g/7½oz plain flour, sieved
1 tsp mixed spice
1 tbsp black treacle
3 tbsps sherry or brandy

1 Mix together the dried fruit, cherries and almonds.
2 Beat together the butter and sugar until pale and creamy.
3 Gradually beat in the egg, beating well between each addition. Add a little of the flour if the mixture begins to curdle.

4 Carefully fold in the flour and spice using a metal spoon, then fold in the fruit.
5 Add the treacle and stir until very well combined.
6 Carefully spoon into a greased 20.5cm/8-inch deep cake tin and level the top.
7 Bake in an oven preheated to 150°C/300°F/Gas Mark 2, for about 2½ hours or until a skewer inserted into the centre comes out clean. Allow to cool completely in the tin.
8 When the cake is completely cold, remove the greaseproof paper and prick the top of the cake with a fine skewer or cocktail stick.
9 Sprinkle the sherry or brandy over the top of the cake and allow this to soak in. Cover with fresh greaseproof paper and seal in an airtight container.

Cook's Notes

Time
Preparation takes about 30 minutes, cooking time is about 2½ hours.

Cook's Tip
The cake will improve in flavour and texture if stored in an airtight container for 1 month before eating.

Index